D0563082

THE ELECTION OF 1976

TK
526
1976
.E 7

THE ELECTION OF 1976

Reports and Interpretations

Gerald M. Pomper
Ross K. Baker
Charles E. Jacob
Wilson Carey McWilliams
Henry A. Plotkin

Marlene M. Pomper, Editor

WITHDRAWN

LIBRARY SERVICES
INDIANA STATE UNIVERSITY
EVANSVILLE

David McKay Company, Inc.
New York

12499-G   GIFT

THE ELECTION OF 1976:

Reports and Interpretations

Copyright © 1977 by David McKay Company, Inc.

All rights reserved, including the right to reproduce
this book, or parts thereof, in any form, except for
the inclusion of brief quotations in a review.

All tables reprinted from the *Congressional
Quarterly* by permission of the publishers.

Manufactured in the United States of America

Developmental Editor: Edward Artinian
Editorial and Design Supervisor: Nicole Benevento
Interior Design: Pencils Portfolio, Inc.
Cover and Jacket Design: Lawrence Ratzkin
Manufacturing and Production Supervisor: Donald W. Strauss
Composition: Fuller Typesetting of Lancaster
Printing and Binding: The Maple Press

Library of Congress Cataloging in Publication Data

Main entry under title:

The Election of 1976.

   Includes bibliographical references and index.
    1. Presidents—United States—Election—
1976—Addresses, essays, lectures.
2. Elections—United States—Addresses, essays,
lectures. I. Pomper, Gerald M.
JK526.E37   329'.023'730925   77–1488
ISBN 0–679–30337–5
ISBN 0–679–30345–6 pbk.

PREFACE

MEN and women often live their lives seeking a perfect time, a brief moment that will provide a matchless experience. This was the quest of Faust, who dreamt of a point in his existence when he could say, "Tarry a while, you are so beautiful."

Faust was a scholar seeking new, sensual experiences. Most scholars must be content with intellectual pursuits. The moments they savor are more commonly historical than personal events. This book is our effort to prolong, through immediate analysis, the exciting election year of 1976.

We lack perspective on these events, yet we believe there are indications that 1976 will be seen as a vital time. Coming amid the national bicentennial, the election inevitably aroused great expectations. The results, too, appear to be significant. Innovations are evident in the ballot results, the nominating patterns, the issues, and the likely policies of the Carter administration.

In the following essays, five political scientists report the results and probe the significance of the election of 1976. As more data become available, we will need to amend our analyses, perhaps even to reject them. Nevertheless, we see value in these quick interpretations. Being close to the events, we have a greater sense of intimacy. Furthermore, in making these quick judgments, we provide a baseline for others and for later, more complete analyses.

As the events of the year proceeded, the political truths of the past were proven inadequate. An unknown candidate was nominated by the Democratic party, while incumbent President Gerald Ford was almost denied renomination by the Republican party. After the national conventions, Jimmy Carter held a lead of more than 30 percent in some public-opinion polls, but almost lost the election.

Yet, even as Ford came close to holding possession of the White House, his party was unable to increase the one-third minority it held in Congress or improve its position in the states. The clamorous, confusing issues of the campaign ranged alphabetically from abortion to Yugoslavia and from the elemental questions of sexual lust to the esoteric questions of nuclear proliferation. The most vital policy questions, however, were the basic and traditional economic issues of unemployment and inflation. In the end, the voters chose change. A new administration would begin America's third century.

In this volume, we seek to report and analyze these events, to gain perspective on the novel aspects of the election of 1976, and to forecast future directions. For the most part, we agree in our interpretations. Where differences exist among us, we must necessarily await future data to test our hypotheses. In the spirit of American political history, we invite our readers to join the debate.

The five authors of this work are members of the political science faculty of Rutgers University:

Ross K. Baker, professor at Rutgers College, is author of *The Afro-American*. He served as a special assistant to Senator Walter Mondale.

Charles E. Jacob, professor and chairman at Rutgers College, is the author of *Policy and Bureaucracy* and co-author of *The Performance of American Government*.

Wilson Carey McWilliams is professor and past chairman at Livingston College. He is author of *The Idea of Fraternity in America*, the winner of a National Historical Society prize.

Henry A. Plotkin is assistant professor at Livingston College and author of the forthcoming book *The American Corporate Order*.

Gerald M. Pomper is professor and graduate director, and a senior research associate of the Center for Policy Research. He is the author of *Elections in America* and *Voters' Choice*.

This volume was produced under severe constraints of time. We are unusually grateful to those who typed the final drafts: Jaki Kalanski, Phyllis Moditz, Anita Neugeboren, Rose Nickas, Betty Van Aiken, and Mary Wilk. Our greatest debt is to our editor, Marlene M. Pomper. She provided whatever coherence, stylistic grace, and clarity is evident in these essays. Ours is the responsibility for the hasty and ill-considered judgments. While certain we have made mistakes, we offer this remembrance of the stirring events of 1976.

December 1976

G.M.P.

CONTENTS

TABLES

The Nominating Contests and Conventions
Gerald M. Pomper

T was obvious.

Before the 1976 presidential nominations, the experts agreed on a number of self-evident truths.

An incumbent President, Gerald Ford, would certainly be nominated without difficulty for a full term. No President since Chester Arthur in 1884 had been denied renomination. Since then, the power and prestige of the office had grown enormously, making it impossible for a party to repudiate the leadership of its most prominent representative.

The Democrats would certainly hold a divisive convention. It was in the nature of Democrats to fight, a congenial characteristic particularly evidenced in the bloody conflicts of Chicago in 1968 and the long convention nights of 1972 in Miami. Moreover, the Democrats apparently were going to guarantee conflict by their insistence on representation for women, youth, and racial minorities, and by their new rules for delegate selection. Symbolic of the upcoming battle was the choice of New York for the convention site, the city in which the Democrats in 1924 took three weeks and 103 ballots to choose a losing presidential nominee.

After the Democrats exhausted themselves, they certainly would select a compromise figure, most likely Hubert Humphrey or Edward Kennedy. Obviously they would not select a southerner, an unknown with no national experience, or a former state governor without an existing power base.

It was obvious—but wrong. In fact, President Ford was renominated only by the slimmest of margins and only after a narrow escape from early defeat. The Democrats held a placid convention with no significant disagreements. For President, they overwhelmingly endorsed Jimmy Carter, a one-term former governor of Georgia. The predictions of the experts failed.[1] With the advantage of hindsight, however, perhaps we can understand what happened, and why.

Before 1976: The Preprimary Period

The cause of the astonishing results of 1976 can be located in various events of the preceding four years. These include the Watergate scandal and resulting federal and state legislation, as well as changes in the parties' rules and organization.

WATERGATE REFORMS

In the middle of the 1972 campaign, a burglary was attempted at the Democratic National Committee headquarters in the Watergate area of Washington, D.C. From this incident developed the greatest scandal in American political history. It led ultimately to the virtual impeachment and resignation of President Richard Nixon. Earlier, Vice-President Spiro Agnew had resigned after the discovery of unrelated corruption.[2] As a result, Gerald Ford was first appointed as vice-president to replace Agnew, and became President on Nixon's departure.

For the first time, the United States had a President with no plausible claim of popular support. The most democratic office in the nation was now filled by a person who had received no votes outside of a single Michigan congressional district. The moral authority of that office had been severely weakened by Nixon and Agnew's conduct, and would be further eroded when the new President issued Nixon a general pardon. Simultaneously, the political power of the Presidency had been weakened by the overreaching actions of its occupants during the Vietnam war, by revelations of repressive actions, and by institutional conflicts with Congress.

"The power of the Presidency moves as a mighty host only *with* the grain of liberty and morality."[3] With lessened democratic, moral, and political authority, Gerald Ford could no longer count on the power of incumbency to assure his nomination to a full term in the White House. Nor could he rely on his personal popularity within the party, for an early poll of Republican county chairmen revealed that Ronald Reagan was heavily preferred over the then Vice-President Ford.[4] The normal expectations of an uncontested nomination took no account of these changed circumstances.

The Watergate scandal led to legislative changes. A basic transformation of American politics began with the new election finance law, passed in 1974, modified and partially voided by the Supreme Court early in 1976, and then reenacted by Congress.[5] Previously, political finance was autonomously controlled by the parties and the candidates, who raised their own funds from whatever sources and in whatever amounts were available, and who spent as much as they had on hand—and often more. No effective restraints existed on either fund raising or spending.

Various abuses were possible, and Watergate revealed that many had occurred. Individual large contributors could expect special favors, such as the raising of price supports for the milk producers who contributed to the Nixon campaign. An imbalance between the resources of the two major parties was possible, as in the 2:1 disparity between the Nixon and McGovern campaigns. Money might be illegally raised from corporations and spent for criminal activities such as the Watergate burglary itself.

The new federal finance laws attempt to meet these problems. They limit individual contributions to $1,000 to any single candidate, and a total of $25,000 for all federal elections. Presidential candidates are provided federal funds to match the first $250 of each contribution, but are limited to specific spending totals in each state, to total expenditures of $10 million in seeking the nomination, and to a total of $20 million in the general election.[6] To obtain these funds, a candidate need only accept the spending limitations and raise an initial sum of at least $5,000 in each of twenty states—a total of $100,000. Beyond these limits on campaigners, the Supreme Court ruled there could not be a limitation on any candidate who did not accept federal subsidies, on congressional candidates, or on individual spending by private citizens that was independent of the parties and candidates.

The presidential nominations were considerably affected by the new laws. Their most important general effect was to facilitate access to the competition, since federal money was now available to persons who could reach a low threshold of private financial support. With "fat cats" essentially written out, candidates who counted on large donations by wealthy persons no longer could overwhelm less well endowed rivals. A greater premium therefore was placed on individual voter contact, on efficient organization, and on support from persons willing to spend their own money independently. Moreover, by directing funds toward candidates rather than toward party organizations, the law weakened the established political organizations and their ability to control the selection of convention delegates.

This trend was reinforced by another development, the spread of state presidential primaries. In 1976, nearly three-fourths of the convention delegates, from thirty states, were chosen directly by the voters, and these delegates typically were then bound to support one of the presidential aspirants. As recently as 1968, primaries were held in only a third of the states, with most delegates selected by internal party processes, such as state conventions, or in nonbinding primaries.

The extension of the primaries had many causes: the reform rules adopted by the parties, especially the Democrats; the reaction to the Watergate scandals; a desire by states to attract media coverage of their local contests; and a long-standing tendency to divorce state and national politics. From these causes critical effects followed. By limiting the power of the state party organizations in delegate selection, the primaries increased the opportunities of an outsider, an insurgent, a media favorite, a personality, even an unknown. Party endorsement came to mean less, but personal organization and personal appeal came to mean more.

PARTY CHANGES

Not only did the Presidency, the finance laws, and state statutes change in the period before the 1976 election. Important alterations also occurred in the two major political parties, preparing the way for the events of the election year.

The Republicans, enjoying the luxury of two consecutive victories, felt no urgency toward reform. Nevertheless, a basic shift in power was underway in the party, which would critically affect the coming race. Once said to be controlled by an "eastern Establishment," the party was coming to reflect more the dominance of the rising industrial and commercial classes of the "Sun Belt," the South, Southwest and Far West.[7] Some of this power shift was inevitable, given the national movement of population and votes. The shift was exaggerated, however, by the distribution of convention delegates.

The party had adopted new apportionment rules that effectively discriminated against the larger states of the Northeast and Midwest. It did so by distributing a third of the total convention seats as "bonus" delegates to any state, regardless of size, that voted Republican for President, the Senate, House, or state governor. The system was challenged by liberal Republicans as a violation of the "one-man, one-vote" principle, but the courts declined to intervene in this party matter.[8] The result was to reduce the power of the older areas of the nation, illustratively decreasing the share of the New England and mid-Atlantic states from the 29.5 percent they enjoyed at the time of the Eisenhower nomination in 1952 to less than a fourth of the 1976 total. This shift in turn would increase the nomination chances of a candidate with particular appeal to the newly emerging areas of the nation.

Changes in the Democratic party were more extensive. Part of the change was essentially one of spirit and temperament. Previously, the party had been sharply divided. George Wallace led a third party in 1968 that gained nearly a seventh of the presidential vote, mostly from Democrats and Independents,[9] and his angry rhetoric made him the leading vote-getter in the 1972 Democratic primaries until his attempted assassination. Other dissidents sought fuller representation for deprived groups, demonstrated for an end to the Vietnam war, pleaded for racial justice, and demanded structural and policy changes in the party. Factionalism and reform swept the party in 1972, bringing sharp increases in the number of women, youth, and minority delegates, a platform pledge of Vietnam withdrawal, the creation of a national party organization, and the insurgent nomination of George McGovern.

After the election, the party quieted; and slowly a general desire to achieve unity and victory became evident. The end of the war removed the most immediate source of internal conflict. The revelations of Watergate provided a common feeling of outrage and persecution. The Democratic sweep in the congressional elections of 1974, encouraging early polls, and the nation's economic downturn indicated that the party stood a good chance of victory in the next election.

In these circumstances, a willingness to compromise or avoid differences became evident. A mid-term party conference was held in 1974, the first in American history, but the only policy issues considered were the economic questions on which Democrats were relatively united; newer and more divisive racial and social issues were shelved.[10] A party charter was also adopted. It simultaneously prohibited discrimination in party affairs, provided for affirmative action programs to encourage minorities, youth, and women, and banned mandatory quotas.[11]

Additionally, the Democrats made a number of changes in convention rules that would eventually affect the character of the 1976 meetings. After adopting its affirmative-action guidelines, the party provided for a Compliance Review Commission, which would review state party implementation of these national rules. By providing early guidance, the new procedure prevented many conflicts, and eventually not a single credentials issue reached the national convention in New York.

Similar early preparation was given to the party platform, which was written after a series of regional hearings and a three-day preconvention meeting of the full platform committee. As a result, only one minor policy matter was left to the convention. The remainder of the party program was satisfactory to all factions, even though it included such pledges as a pardon for Vietnam war resisters and support of the equal rights amendment, the Supreme Court's abortion ruling, national health insurance, and a federal job guarantee. The process of unifying the party was facilitated by a new rule that limited minority reports to those supported by at least a fourth of the committee.

For the presidential candidates, the most vital changes made by the Democrats were in the means of selecting delegates. New party rules provided that all aspirants for convention delegate—either in primaries or state caucuses—must declare their presidential preference. In this way, voters would find it easy to support their presidential candidates. With most delegates pledged in advance, the opportunity for convention bargaining was reduced.

More vital still was a provision for proportional representation in each state, so that the delegates would closely represent the distribution of candidate preferences among the electorate. The intention, and effect, of this change was to eliminate "winner-take-all" systems, such as that in California, in which the candidate receiving the largest number of votes—even if less than a majority—won all the delegates from that state. The same rule of proportional representation applied to states choosing delegates in party caucuses and conventions.

Two effects would follow. First, a candidate could benefit even from a losing tally, for he would still receive some delegates and would not be completely shut out. Second, this change could drastically reduce the influence of the traditional "power brokers" of the larger states, who possessed sizable unified blocs of delegates that could be moved from one candidate to another. The spread of primaries threatened the control of these persons directly, as did the new rules opening caucuses to nonpoliticians. Even if powerful individuals were able to dominate a state convention or primary, they no longer would have exclusive control of an entire delegation. Minority preferences also would be heard, and thereby lessen the impact of a unified state.

Underlying all these detailed rules was a basic transformation of the Democrats into a truly national association. Previously the party was no more than the traditional collection of state factions which gathered every four years to agree on a temporary standard-bearer. Now the Democrats were altering their character, sometimes deliberately, sometimes unknowingly, into a coherent organization. They had begun with the imposition of a loyalty oath in 1956 and the prohibition of racial discrimination in 1964.[12] They had required new delegate selection procedures in 1968 and 1972, and revised these rules for 1976. They had created permanent legislative, executive, and judicial institutions in their innovative 1974 charter. Their representatives had written a 1976 party program acceptable to all. Within the Democratic party, these new national tides were eroding the position of the established local baronies and islands of power. In turn, the Democratic party was leading the nationalization of American politics.

1976: The Nominations

Candidates, like other men, are guided more by their perceptions, "the pictures in their heads," than by objective reality. As the contestants entered the 1976 nominating lists, we can now see how inappropriate were almost all their strategies.

THE DEMOCRATIC ALSO-RANS
By the beginning of 1976, there were a dozen serious presidential candidates in the Democratic party. Ideologically they ranged from

the racial conservatism of George Wallace to the forthright liberalism of Morris Udall, and they differed as well in their biographies and political experience. With the exception of Jimmy Carter, they shared one basic characteristic: Like the typical military leader, they were fighting previous wars, not preparing for the current struggle.

Each of the initial front-runners seemed fixated by an earlier Democratic nomination, usually one in which he was prominently involved. Thus, Henry Jackson, senator from Washington and the early leader, appeared to hark back to the successful campaign of John Kennedy in 1960. Kennedy had built a talented personal organization, accumulated considerable funds from family and friends before the first primaries, and struck important alliances with major groups within the party, including some labor unions and urban machines. Carefully selecting his testing grounds, he won seven successive primaries, and then used his demonstrated popularity to gain the allegiance of the party organizations in the large industrial states of New York, Illinois, and Pennsylvania.[13]

Jackson in 1960 served as the Democratic national chairman, and his own 1976 campaign bore this historical imprint. He accumulated $2.8 million before the new contribution limits became effective, sought the early informal endorsement of labor and major state organizations, and planned a limited primary effort. By winning in such major industrial states as Massachusetts, New York, and Pennsylvania, Jackson expected to start a bandwagon that would bring him the nomination.[14]

Hubert Humphrey, a real but unannounced candidate, apparently remembered the 1968 campaign. In that year of Vietnam travail, the vice-president had left the primaries to Eugene McCarthy, Robert Kennedy, and stand-ins for the administration. He had relied on the power of the incumbents, his personal following in the state party organizations, and the unacceptability of McCarthy and unavailability of Edward Kennedy.[15] In the current battle, Humphrey hoped the Democrats, in a deadlocked convention, would again turn to him, the acceptable elder statesman of the party. He traveled widely, effectively arguing for the party, but never openly on his own behalf, while acknowledging his readiness to accept the nomination. By encouraging many candidates to enter the contest, he hoped to promote the convention divisions that would lead to his own selection.

George Wallace remembered the 1972 nomination. Paralyzed below the waist from an assassination attempt, the Alabama governor took comfort in memories of the fanatic crowds that had greeted him in 1972, in the string of primary victories that he accumulated from Florida to Michigan, and the deference paid to him at and after the Miami convention. Amply endowed with funds raised through direct mail from millions of small contributors, Wallace again expected a mass revolt to bring him dollars—now matched by the federal government—primary votes, delegates, and a major voice in the convention maneuvering, if not the nomination itself. Wallace's expectations were in fact shared by other Democrats. A major reason for the abolition of the winner-take-all primaries was to dilute the anticipated impact of Wallace pluralities.

Memories of 1972 excited other Democrats as well. Morris Udall, congressman from Arizona, was one of a number of liberals who attempted to repeat the success of George McGovern in 1972. Aided by widespread resistance to continued American involvement in Vietnam, and bolstered by new party rules written under his leadership, Senator McGovern had then won delegates in newly open party caucuses and accumulated a string of primary victories. Early successes then snowballed, bringing him contributions from large and small donors, and surging popularity in both the polls and primaries.[16] Like McGovern in 1972, Udall in 1976 began with little public recognition. He too hoped to become the candidate of the left, to attract money that would be doubled by the federal subsidies, and thus to develop the momentum that would make him and the liberal faction victorious. But Udall, and other liberals such as Fred Harris and Birch Bayh, lacked an emotional issue such as Vietnam. They could not expect the same outpouring of amateur enthusiasm that had led to McGovern's nomination.

None of these Democratic candidates recognized the new political terrain on which they fought. The spread of primaries, requirements of proportional representation, and public avowals of the delegates' preferences meant that strategies limited to a few states would throw away prospective votes. An emphasis on older power groups, such as the AFL–CIO and the urban machines, neglected the rise of new interests, such as the coalition of nine unions active in the Labor Coalition Clearinghouse. Strategies relying on large contributions failed to take account of the new federal laws. An emphasis on specific issues neglected the shift to new concerns, particularly the general American discontent, after Watergate, with all institutions of government.

THE DEMOCRATS: CARTER

Jimmy Carter, unencumbered by memories of a previous nomination effort, avoided most errors. Aware of the shifting of population and power, he grasped the possibility of a southerner winning nomination for the first time since slavery rent the Union. Only the racial issue had barred southern access to the White House, but Carter could present himself as an advocate of racial equality, and would be aided in that presentation by respected blacks such as Martin Luther King, Sr., and Congressman Andrew Young.

Carter grasped as well the strategic implications of the new party rules. With delegates available everywhere, it was desirable to make an effort in all states. The Georgian's supporters were evident in every caucus, and the candidate was entered in all but one state primary. New spending limits and the lack of large contributions meant that he could not rely on expensive mass media for his campaign. Instead, personal organization was stressed.

After gaining the position of chairman of the Democrats' 1974 campaign committee, Carter traveled throughout the nation, aiding Democratic aspirants while establishing a personal network in every state. Where traditional party organizations remained strong, as in Chicago, he avoided confrontation. Where they were weakening, as in Pennsylvania, he struck alliances with new men of power, such as Mayor Peter Flaherty of Pittsburgh. After the 1974 election, Carter's term as governor of Georgia ended, leaving him free to concentrate exclusively on the nominating campaign. All other contestants continued to have official duties.[17]

The Georgian's initial problem was that he was unknown and not taken seriously. He appeared unrecognized on the popular television program "What's My Line?" in 1973, and was barely mentioned in the early national opinion polls. This obscurity was obviously not fatal and even carried a perverse advantage. Carter, able to leave his "disposable" occupation [18] as a farm businessman in family hands, could travel and organize without arousing concern from his future opponents.

Given the general skepticism, any early success by Carter would be magnified in its impact. Intensive organizing brought such a success, when the Georgian came in first in local Iowa caucuses, the first step in the nation toward the selection of delegates. By vigorous personal campaigning, he was then able to lead the field in the first primary in New Hampshire, with 28 percent of the Democratic vote. This victory meant only that a mere 23,000 persons had chosen Carter. Nevertheless, the vote ended skepticism about his effort. Its effect, in fact, was exaggerated by the mass media. Always viewing politics as just another horse race, they quickly labeled Carter as the "front runner" on the basis of these first limited results. Cover photos on national magazines, television interviews, and increasing popular attention followed.

The Carter campaign also benefited from its approach to policy issues. Unlike the contests of 1968 and 1972, there was no single dominating issue such as Vietnam, but rather a diffusion of interest among issues. Carter responded to this situation. Contrary to many criticisms, Carter did not lack policy positions, and prepared sixty relatively specific programs on topics ranging from Cyprus to national health insurance. The party platform incorporated many of these proposals.

While not evading issues, Carter did not emphasize them in his campaign. His stress was on asserted personal qualities of honesty, competence, and trustworthiness. He correctly sensed that in the aftermath of the social upheavals, corruption, and alienation of previous years, the voters were seeking a means to revive their underlying trust and affection for American government. The electorate wanted to express—in the best sense of the word—its patriotism, its basic love of country. Carter expressed these sentiments repeatedly in his campaign and in his acceptance speech. "We want to have faith again! We want to be proud again! We *just* want the truth again! . . . We can have an American government that's turned away from scandal and corruption and official cynicism and is once again as decent and competent as our people." [19]

On the more specific issues, Carter's stands were generally those of a moderate liberal within the Democratic party tradition.* Of greater importance than any particular topic, however, was his ability to satisfy important issue constituencies within the party. Blacks constituted a large bloc of support that was particularly important to a southern white. Advocates of newer social mores were pacified by his support of the equal rights amendment and his acceptance of the Supreme Court's abortion decision. On the emotional and symbolic question of amnesty for Vietnam war re-

* See chapter 2 for an extended analysis of the campaign issues.

sisters, Carter was able to defuse the issue by supporting a "pardon" rather than amnesty. Economic liberals were satisfied by his support of such legislation as federal guarantees of employment.

Through such tactics and stands, the governor was able to win support over a broad spectrum of the party. In Pennsylvania's primary, illustratively, he gained identical pluralities among both those who agreed and disagreed that the government should promote housing integration.[20] By the time of the last primary in Ohio, he won both half of the Democrats who supported McGovern before the 1972 convention and half of the Democrats who defected to Richard Nixon in that year's general election.[21] Up to the time of the convention, at least, most voters were unclear on Carter's issue positions. The lack of clarity was not decisive, however, for Carter's backers particularly emphasized the personal qualities they sought in a candidate, and they were sufficiently numerous to bring him the nomination.[22]

Despite these advantages, Carter's success should not be seen as inevitable, even with the advantage of quarterbacking this political game after the final whistle. Success came from skill, from the effect of new rules, and also from luck and strategic errors by the other candidates.

The general pattern of the preconvention campaign was one of the successive elimination of candidates. McGovern had followed a similar course in 1972, but his campaign was focused on the left of the party and came to fruition by removing the centrist candidates. By contrast in 1976, Carter's campaign was clearly centrist and triumphed by successively eliminating candidates from the more extreme factions.

The elimination process began early, with the liberal ranks thinned by the early withdrawals of Birch Bayh and Sargent Shriver, following the Massachusetts primary. Carter took the most vital steps toward victory in Florida and North Carolina, where his triumphs over George Wallace effectively eliminated the right-wing threat to the party, secured the South as a base for Carter, and reduced the likelihood of a deadlocked convention. After a weak showing in New York, the Georgian defeated Jackson in Pennsylvania, destroying the Washington senator's strategy. When Hubert Humphrey declined to enter the last available primary, in New Jersey, Carter faced only the scattered opposition of Morris Udall and two new entrants, Frank Church and Edmund Brown. A series of narrow victories over Udall in Wisconsin, Michigan, and

South Dakota made the Arizona congressman's campaign unviable. While the remaining candidates contested one another, Carter continued to amass delegates in all regions. With his decisive victory in the last primary in Ohio, Carter was assured of the nomination. His opponents had fought with too little, too late.

At several points in the preconvention period, the Carter campaign suffered setbacks: a fourth-place finish in the Massachusetts primary, the open invitation of New Jersey Democrats to Hubert Humphrey to enter a state where reliable polls showed him with a strong lead, the late victories of Church and Brown. The Georgian was able to recover from these setbacks because they were only temporary. Thus, the Massachusetts defeat was followed in a week by the Florida victory. Carter also gained from the mistakes of his competitors. The New Jersey invitation was declined by Senator Humphrey, who thereby lost his last opportunity to demonstrate popular support. Similarly, Governor Brown, although winning a preference vote in Maryland, lost almost all the delegates to Carter because he did not meet the necessary filing requirements.

Even in defeat, Carter won. In the last three weeks of the primaries, twelve state contests were held, of which Carter lost five. Nevertheless, he gained a proportionate share of the delegates even in these losing states. At the same time, he was gaining a much larger number of delegates in less publicized, less contentious primaries, particularly in the South. Tennessee had been conceded to Carter, so little attention was paid to the fact that he was assured of 36 delegates there on the same day his opponents gained only 22 in the heralded Oregon contest. On that day, May 25, Carter won only three of the six primaries, but he gained 107 of the 179 delegates chosen.

The overall impact of the primaries can be seen in table 1.1, which shows the results in chronological order. More important than individual races is the cumulative effect, presented in the last three columns. These data show, for each state, the combined national and Carter votes up to that date, and the current Carter percentage of the total vote in the primaries.[23] The impressive feature of these data is how Carter reached and held an early position as the preferred candidate of some 40 percent of the voters. The publicized "defeats" by Church and Brown caused hardly any change.

At the same time, Carter was quickly rising in the public-opinion polls as the choice of all Democrats. While preferred by only 4

Table 1.1

The Democratic Primaries of 1976 _____

		State	
Date	State	Total vote	Carter vote
Feb. 24	New Hampshire *	82,381	23,373
March 2	Massachusetts	735,821	101,948
	Vermont	38,714	16,335
March 9	Florida *	1,300,330	448,844
March 16	Illinois *	1,311,914	630,915
March 23	North Carolina *	604,832	324,437
April 6	New York ᵃ		
	Wisconsin *	740,528	271,220
April 27	Pennsylvania *	1,385,042	511,905
May 1	Texas * ᵃ		
May 4	Alabama ᵃ		
	Dis. of Columbia *	24,582	9,759
	Georgia *	502,371	419,172
	Indiana *	614,361	417,463
May 11	Nebraska	175,013	65,833
	West Virginia ᵇ	372,577	—
May 18	Maryland	591,746	219,404
	Michigan *	708,666	307,559
May 25	Arkansas *	501,800	314,306
	Idaho	74,405	8,818
	Kentucky *	306,006	181,690
	Nevada	75,242	17,567
	Oregon	432,622	115,310
	Tennessee *	334,078	259,243
June 1	Montana	106,841	26,329
	Rhode Island	60,348	18,237
	South Dakota *	58,671	24,186
June 8	New Jersey	360,839	210,655
	Ohio *	1,118,288	593,130
	California	3,373,732	690,171

* Designates states in which Carter placed first in preference vote of delegates.

ᵃ States not holding preference vote and not included in cumulative totals. Carter percentage is of delegates selected.

ᵇ Carter not in primary. Vote not included in cumulative totals.

percent of party identifiers in January, Carter reached a virtual tie with Hubert Humphrey among Democrats by early April, and became the clear favorite of over 40 percent in May and June. At the same pace, he was rising in delegate commitments, achieving close

		Cumulative	
Carter %	*Total vote*	*Carter vote*	*Carter %*
28.4	82,381	23,373	28.4
13.9			
42.2	856,916	141,656	16.5
34.5	2,157,272	590,500	27.4
48.1	3,469,186	1,221,415	35.2
53.6	4,074,018	1,545,852	37.9
12.8			
36.6	4,814,546	1,817,072	37.7
37.0	6,199,588	2,328,977	37.6
93.9			
8.6			
39.7			
83.4			
68.0	7,340,902	3,175,371	43.2
37.6	7,515,915	3,241,204	43.1
—			
37.1			
43.4	8,816,327	3,768,167	42.7
62.6			
11.9			
59.4			
23.3			
26.7			
77.6	10,540,480	4,665,101	44.2
24.6			
30.2			
41.2	10,766,340	4,733,853	44.0
58.4			
52.3	12,245,467	5,537,638	45.2
20.5	15,619,199	6,277,809	39.9

to 40 percent even by conservative estimates, with no opponent reaching even half his total.[24]

Past convention history has shown that a candidate receiving over 40 percent of delegate roll-call votes will surely go on to win the nomination.[25] In the new system of nomination, popular support is more important for convention maneuvering. A candidate winning 40 percent in primary votes and opinion polls, especially in a crowded field, is likely to be victorious.

With the presidential nomination won by Carter by the time of the Ohio primary, the Democratic convention was unusually harmonious. The month before the meeting was taken up by a succession of endorsements of the governor by his former rivals and the erstwhile power brokers of the party, by compromising on various credentials and platform issues, and by Carter's well-publicized search for an appropriate vice-presidential candidate.

The single roll call for the presidential nomination, presented in table 1.2, demonstrated the scope of Carter's victory, giving him

Table 1.2

Democratic Presidential Nomination Roll Call

State	Delegate votes	Carter	Udall	Brown	Wallace	Others
Alabama	35	30			5	
Alaska	10	10				
Arizona	25	6	19			
Arkansas	26	25	1			
California	280	73	2	205		
Colorado	35	15	6	11		3
Connecticut	51	35	16			
Delaware	12	10.50		1.50		
Florida	81	70		1	10	
Georgia	50	50				
Hawaii	17	17				
Idaho	16	16				
Illinois	169	164	1	2	1	1
Indiana	75	72			3	
Iowa	47	25	20	1		1
Kansas	34	32	2			
Kentucky	46	39	2		5	
Louisiana	41	18		18	5	
Maine	20	15	5			
Maryland	53	44	6	3		
Massachusetts	104	65	21		11	7
Michigan	133	75	58			
Minnesota	65	37	2	1		25
Mississippi	24	23				
Missouri	71	58	4	2		7

Table 1.2 (continued)

State	Delegate Votes	Carter	Udall	Brown	Wallace	Others
Montana	17	11	2			4
Nebraska	23	20		3		
Nevada	11	3		6.50		1.50
New Hampshire	17	15	2			
New Jersey	108	108				
New Mexico	18	14	4			
New York	274	209.50	56.50	4		4
North Carolina	61	56			3	
North Dakota	13	13				
Ohio	152	132	20			
Oklahoma	37	32	1			4
Oregon	34	16		10		8
Pennsylvania	178	151	21	6		
Rhode Island	22	14		8		
South Carolina	31	28		1	2	
South Dakota	17	11	5			1
Tennessee	46	45			1	
Texas	130	124		4	1	1
Utah	18	10		5		3
Vermont	12	5	4	3		
Virginia	54	48	6			
Washington	53	36	11	3		3
West Virginia	33	30	1			2
Wisconsin	68	29	25		10	4
Wyoming	10	8	1	1		
District of Columbia	17	12	5			
Puerto Rico	22	22				
Canal Zone	3	3				
Guam	3	3				
Virgin Islands	3	3				
Democrats Abroad	3	2.50		.50		
Totals	3,008	2,238.50	329.50	300.50	57	79.50

SOURCE: *Congressional Quarterly Weekly Report* 34 (17 July 1976): 1873.

nearly three-fourths of the total votes. Only Udall and Brown did not release their pledged delegates before the tally, but they joined in the general party unity. The last echoes of past efforts were evident in the handful of votes for Humphrey, Jackson, and Wallace. This roll call lacked the emotions of uncertainty, for it did no more than record formally a predestined result. It did well represent the underlying drama of the transfer of power in a transformed party.

THE REPUBLICANS

In contrast to Democratic unity, the Republicans seemed intent on self-destruction. Division within the GOP was certainly perverse. By 1976, polls estimated that only a fifth of the nation identified with the party. If interested in winning a majority, the party could not further shrink this shriveled foundation. It could succeed only by solidifying its base, and then adding substantial numbers of Independents and Democrats.

Moreover, a contest in the Republican party seemed not only unwise but also unlikely. As opposed to the Democrats, Republicans were relatively unified on the basic political issues. Thus, in the Republican ranks, conservatives outnumbered liberals by a 2–1 margin, while among Democrats the proportions of the two ideological groups were almost equal.[26] Furthermore, the Republicans possessed the White House, and had an obvious candidate in President Ford. His popularity was not overwhelming, to be sure, but his record was apparently acceptable to much of the electorate, for he ran close to or ahead of potential Democratic opponents in the polls. Among members of his own party, certainly, the President seemed secure, winning the support of up to 61 percent of party identifiers in 1975.[27]

In the event, the President did secure his nomination. But he did so with only 52.5 percent of the delegates, with the outcome in doubt until the actual convention roll calls (see table 1.3). Eventually the party fulfilled normal expectations, but only after an astonishing contest. An explanation is needed then, not of Ford's success, but of Reagan's virtual victory.

Part of the explanation lies in the factors previously discussed. Watergate damaged the prestige and authority of the Presidency, making incumbency of less value for Ford. Its worth was further diminished by the new President's pardon of Nixon and by a shift of voter concern away from foreign affairs, the area of greatest presidential prestige. The new finance laws removed one of the major advantages of a President, his access to large financial contributors. Reagan could now seek an equal financial footing, and the federal government would subsidize his insurgent campaign against that government's chief executive. Moreover, restrictions on spending benefited the former California governor, for they required emphasis on personal contacts rather than media advertising. Reagan had developed these contacts in years of lecturing to conservative and party groups. Since he held no office, moreover, Reagan was free to campaign nationally for nearly two years, while Ford had to meet the unfamiliar and difficult demands of the Presidency.

Changes in the formal rules also worked to the Californian's advantage. The shift in apportionment favored a candidate with his particular appeal to the South and Far West. The effect of this change is seen in the last two columns of table 1.3, where the actual vote in 1976 is recalculated to resemble the distribution of support in the 1952 Republican contest. In this recalculation, the votes apportioned to each state in 1952 are divided between Ford and Reagan in the same proportions they actually received in 1976. Under the old apportionment, Ford would have been a comfortable winner with 56.5 percent of the delegates. His more narrow victory in the real contest of 1976 is due to the relative loss of delegates by the East and Midwest to the South and Far West.[28]

The spread of presidential primaries also favored Reagan. Party leaders became less influential in the choice of delegates. Instead, an effective campaigner like Reagan could make a direct popular appeal, and actually outpoll the President in these contests. Reagan also gained by the continuation of "winner-take-all" primaries in the Republican party. Victory in California alone brought the governor 167 delegates. If the Democrats' new practice of proportional representation had been followed, Reagan would have won only 108 to Ford's 59, a much smaller margin.

Policy issues brought Reagan further advantages. The Californian was openly ideological, forcefully advocating a series of conservative positions including reduced federal involvement in the economy, reliance on military solutions to foreign problems, and opposition to social innovations such as school busing and abortion. Ford's positions were hardly different, but he did not place the same emphasis on this conservative ideology; moreover, Ford was required to compromise his beliefs at times in dealing with a Democratic Congress. Enjoying the luxury of nonresponsibility, Reagan could appeal directly to the ideological preferences of conservative voters. His stands were likely to be particularly favored by Republican party activists, who have been consistently even more conservative than the party's rank and file.[29]

Reagan also was able to draw some support across party lines, especially after the Democratic contest turned into a Carter rout. Conservative Democrats who had planned to vote for Wallace, or

Table 1.3

Republican Convention Votes

State	Votes	1976 Rules vote	
		Yes (Pro-Reagan)	*No (Pro-Ford)*
Alabama	37	37	
Alaska	19	2	17
Arizona	29	25	4
Arkansas	27	17	10
California	167	166	1
Colorado	31	26	5
Connecticut	35		35
Delaware	17	1	16
D.C.	14		14
Florida	66	28	38
Georgia	48	38	7
Guam	4		4
Hawaii	19	1	18
Idaho	21	17	4
Illinois	101	20	79
Indiana	54	27	27
Iowa	36	18	18
Kansas	34	4	30
Kentucky	37	26	10
Louisiana	41	34	6
Maine	20	5	15
Maryland	43	8	35
Massachusetts	43	15	28
Michigan	84	29	55
Minnesota	42	5	35
Mississippi	30		30
Missouri	49	30	18
Montana	20	20	
Nebraska	25	18	7
Nevada	18	15	3
New Hampshire	21	3	18
New Jersey	67	4	62
New Mexico	21	20	1
New York	154	20	134
North Carolina	54	51	3
North Dakota	18	6	12
Ohio	97	7	90
Oklahoma	36	36	
Oregon	30	14	16

1976 President		President–1952 apportionment	
Ford	Reagan	Ford	Reagan
	37		14.00
17	2	2.68	.32
2	27	0.95	13.05
10	17	4.07	6.93
	167		70.00
5	26	2.90	15.10
35		22.00	
15	2	10.58	1.42
14		6.00	
43	23	11.72	6.28
	48		17.00
4			
18	1	7.58	0.42
4	17	2.66	11.34
86	14	51.36	8.64
9	45	5.31	26.69
19	17	13.70	12.30
30	4	19.40	2.60
19	18	10.26	9.74
5	36	1.82	13.18
15	5	12.00	4.00
43		24.00	
28	15	24.74	13.26
55	29	30.08	15.92
32	10	21.31	6.69
16	14	2.66	2.34
18	31	9.54	16.46
	20		8.00
7	18	5.04	12.96
5	13	3.32	8.68
18	3	12.00	2.00
63	4	35.72	2.28
	21		14.00
133	20	83.14	12.86
25	29	12.01	13.99
11	7	8.55	5.45
91	6	52.53	3.47
	36		16.00
16	14	9.59	8.41

Table 1.3 (continued)

| State | Votes | 1976 Rules vote | |
		Yes (Pro-Reagan)	No (Pro-Ford)
Pennsylvania	103	14	89
Puerto Rico	8		8
Rhode Island	19		19
South Carolina	36	25	11
South Dakota	20	11	9
Tennessee	43	17	26
Texas	100	100	
Utah	20	20	
Vermont	18		18
Virginia	51	36	15
Virgin Islands	4		4
Washington	38	31	7
West Virginia	28	12	16
Wisconsin	45		45
Wyoming	17	9	8
Total	2,259	1,068	1,180

SOURCE: *Congressional Quarterly Weekly Report* 34 (21 August 1976): 2313.

Independents seeking to exert some influence, began to vote in Republican primaries, and to vote for Reagan, the more openly conservative candidate. This Reagan appeal partially neutralized the continued Ford popularity among members of his own party. The President almost always led in the preferences of Republicans, reaching a 62–33 advantage in April, and still maintained a 50–43 lead at the time of the convention. Among other voters, however, his popularity was consistently lower.[30]

There were three distinct phases to the Republican nominating campaign (see table 1.4). For the first months of the year, President Ford gradually developed a leading position. He won narrowly in the initial contested primaries of New Hampshire and Florida, and more substantially over limited opposition in Massachusetts, Illinois, and Wisconsin. By the end of April, Ford had gained almost half the committed delegates, almost three times the Reagan strength, and had reserve strength among uncommitted delegates in New York and Pennsylvania.

1976 President		President–1952 apportionment	
Ford	Reagan	Ford	Reagan
93	10	63.14	6.86
8		3.00	
19		8.00	
9	27	1.50	4.50
9	11	6.30	7.70
21	22	9.76	10.24
	100		38.00
	20		14.00
18		12.00	
16	35	7.20	15.80
4		1.00	
7	31	4.42	19.58
20	8	11.42	4.58
45		30.00	
7	10	4.93	7.07
1,187	1,070	681.89	524.11

To this point, Reagan's success had been limited to a single primary victory in North Carolina. Now the scene of battle shifted to states in which Reagan was stronger, and to states permitting crossover votes by conservative Democrats and Independents. Reagan thus took all of Texas' delegates, surprised observers by winning the vast preponderance of the Indiana vote, and made further gains in caucus states. By the middle of May, with half the delegates chosen, Reagan had become the front-runner.

In the final period before the convention, the President recovered from his losing position, particularly aided by primary victories in Michigan and Maryland. The contest became closer each week. In the final primaries, Reagan's sweep of California was balanced by Ford victories in Ohio and New Jersey. With all but a tenth of the delegates selected, each candidate had gained the once-magic 40 percent that had historically led to nomination bandwagons. But neither bandwagon could roll in this race.

As the last delegates were chosen in state conventions, the Re-

Table 1.4
Republican Primary Results

		State			
Date	State [a]	Ford vote	Reagan vote	Ford %	Reagan %
Feb. 24	New Hampshire	54,824	53,507	50.6	49.4
March 2	Massachusetts	114,042	62,951	64.4	35.6
March 9	Florida	318,844	282,618	53.0	47.0
March 16	Illinois	450,812	307,305	59.5	40.5
March 23	North Carolina	88,249	100,984	46.6	53.4
April 6	Wisconsin	326,081	261,579	55.5	44.5
May 4	Georgia	58,902	127,629	31.6	68.4
	Indiana	303,679	320,356	48.7	51.3
May 11	Nebraska	93,683	112,481	45.4	54.6
	W. Virginia	82,281	62,975	56.6	43.4
May 18	Maryland	94,779	68,910	57.9	42.1
	Michigan	689,540	363,797	65.5	34.5
May 25	Arkansas	11,449	20,209	36.2	63.8
	Idaho	22,200	66,415	25.0	75.0
	Kentucky	67,868	62,567	52.0	48.0
	Nevada	13,767	31,616	30.3	69.7
	Oregon	146,911	133,242	52.4	47.6
	Tennessee	120,564	118,394	50.4	49.6
	Montana	30,814	55,636	35.6	64.4
June 1	Rhode Island	9,341	4,419	67.9	32.1
	South Dakota	36,873	42,967	46.2	53.8
June 8	Ohio	545,770	419,169	56.6	43.4
	California	800,572	1,536,400	34.3	65.7

[a] Uncontested primaries in New Jersey, Pennsylvania, Vermont, and the District of Columbia are excluded, as are the pure delegate selection primaries of Alabama, New York, and Texas. Scattered votes for others are not included.

publican contest came to resemble a sudden-death playoff. The proportion of delegates pledged to Ford stood at 47.9 percent, and to Reagan 45.4 percent. The total vote in the contested primaries revealed a similarly slight advantage for Reagan, who drew ahead with the final race in California.[31] The nomination would be decided by a relative handful of uncommitted delegates; one report estimated that as few as sixteen wavering representatives, out of a total of 2,259, would decide the leadership of the party of Lincoln.[32]

Ultimately, the President won narrowly. He was aided by Rea-

| | Cumulative | | |
Ford vote	Reagan vote	Ford %	Reagan %
54,824	53,507	50.6	49.4
168,866	116,458	59.2	40.8
487,710	399,076	55.0	45.0
938,522	706,381	57.1	42.9
1,026,771	807,365	56.0	44.0
1,352,852	1,068,944	55.9	44.1
1,715,433	1,516,929	53.1	46.9
1,891,397	1,692,385	52.8	47.2
2,675,716	2,125,092	55.7	44.3
3,089,289	2,613,171	54.2	45.8
3,135,503	2,660,557	54.1	45.9
3,681,273	3,079,726	54.4	45.6
4,481,845	4,616,126	49.3	50.7

gan himself, who made the tactical error of endorsing Richard Schweiker, a liberal senator from Pennsylvania, for vice-president, thereby enraging a number of conservative delegates. The President also employed the powers of his office, inviting delegates to the White House and to official functions, giving a sympathetic ear to appeals for local sewerage plants and other official favors, and appearing frequently on televised news programs.

The most vital asset of the Presidency, however, had already been lost: its aura of invincibility. When Ford began to move down in polls, primaries, and committed delegates, the majesty of the office was debilitated. In the Democratic contest, Carter's campaign had built steadily upward and thereby developed an appearance of inevitability. Ford's campaign began on this assumption, since all believed that Presidents do not lose. But, "it is much safer to be feared than loved, if one must choose." Once Ford began to slip, the Republican delegates no longer needed to fear the power of his office. Thus the President almost learned Machiavelli's truth: "Any prince, trusting only in [men's] words and having no other preparations made, will fall to his ruin." [33]

Thus weakened, Ford could not be certain of his nomination even as the Republican convention opened in August. He would first need to win a crucial test vote on the party rules. The Reagan forces proposed that each presidential candidate be required to name his vice-presidential running mate before the first nomination tally. Reagan had already selected Senator Schweiker and now hoped to force the President to make a similar early decision, and thereby to deprive him of possibly bargaining for votes with the enticement of the vice-presidency. The proposed rules change was narrowly defeated, 1068–1180.

The Ford victory on this test vote was closely paralleled in the nomination vote on the following night. In these votes, a regional split was generally evident, with considerable presidential strength in the East and Midwest, more limited support in the South, and virtually none in the Far West. This alignment partially resembled that of past Republican factionalism,[34] but there were many important changes as well. California emerged as a conservative bastion, while the Midwest appeared relatively more liberal than in the past.

The conservative element of the party did not succeed in winning the presidential nomination, but it did effectively dominate the convention. Many concessions were made to its policy positions in the party platform. Traditional moral positions such as opposition to abortion were incorporated. More significantly, a foreign policy plank was added on the floor of the convention that was obliquely critical of the Ford administration's policy of détente with the Soviet Union. Rather than risk a loss, the President's supporters meekly accepted the criticism, so that Ford would now be running on a platform that found his conduct in office partially flawed.

The desire to conciliate the conservatives was evident in other actions of the convention. The most conservative of the potential

running mates, Robert Dole, was selected as vice-president, on the
recommendation of Reagan. The Californian was given the un-
precedented opportunity to address the convention after the President's own acceptance speech, thereby reducing the attention given
to Ford. In his own address, the President emphasized his conservative record: "For two years, I have stood for all the people against
the vote-hungry, free-spending congressional majority on Capitol
Hill . . . I am against the big tax spender and for the little tax-
payer." [35] The Republicans had nominated Gerald Ford. But in
narrowly endorsing its President for a full term, the party was also
establishing its ideological identity.

THE RUNNING MATES

In both parties, the 1976 conventions were innovative in their
selections of the vice-presidential candidate. Since the time of John
Adams, the office had been neglected and ridiculed. As Mr. Dooley
wrote, "It isn't a crime exactly. Ye can't be sint to jail f'r it, but it's
a kind of disgrace. It's like writin' anonymous letters." [36] Nominations were made hastily, usually on command of the presidential
nominee, and typically to provide an ideological or geographical
balance to the national ticket.

By 1976, such disdain for the office had become a clear and
present danger to the nation. Lack of concern for the vice-presidency had led to the casual Republican designation of Spiro Agnew
in 1968 and the hurried Democratic selection of Thomas Eagleton
in 1972. Agnew later resigned from office after the revelation of
his evasion of income taxes, and Eagleton resigned from the ticket
after the revelation of treatment for mental illness. These events
demonstrated that better means were needed for selection of a
running mate. The elevation of Ford from appointed vice-president
to chief executive further accentuated the need for reform.

For the Democrats, Carter engaged in a long deliberate process
before recommending Walter Mondale, senator from Minnesota,
on the last day of the convention. He began with a list of over a
dozen prospective nominees, and later shortened it to seven prospects. A panel of advisers was constituted to screen the possibilities;
research was conducted on their backgrounds; the final aspirants
completed a questionnaire on their health, finances, and personal
lives; and each aspirant was interviewed by the staff and then by
Carter. The total impression created by this process was that of a

serious recruitment of a major executive rather than the traditionally hasty selection of an inoffensive ghost.

Like all presidential candidates, Carter claimed that competence would be the guiding criterion in selection of his running mate. Like other candidates, however, he also kept political considerations in mind, seeking a candidate who would bring some geographical balance to the ticket and help to unify the party. Mondale, the preference of labor and ideological liberals, met these needs. The deliberate pattern of selection further aided Carter's election effort, by presenting a public image of a careful but decisive leader.

The Carter procedure met many of the reforms proposed at this time in a study of the Kennedy Institute of Politics.[37] Yet the Democratic nominee went even further than these academic recommendations. In announcing his endorsement of Mondale, the Georgian called for a basic change in the scheduling of the vice-presidential nomination. The Kennedy Institute study, along with an earlier Democratic party commission,[38] recommended only that an additional day or two be provided between the time of the two nominations. Carter proposed that there be a thirty-day adjournment after the presidential nomination, to allow time for full investigation and deliberation.[39] If followed in the future, this procedure would allow future candidates to exercise the same care, and create the same public interest, as Carter did in 1976.

Innovation was evident in the Republican party as well. Three weeks before the party's convention opened, Ronald Reagan designated Senator Schweiker as his prospective running mate and challenged President Ford to make his preference known early. Furthermore, the Reagan forces attempted to write this new procedure into the party rules, leading to the decisive roll-call vote of the convention.

The prior announcement of the selected candidate followed some reform proposals, but the designation was not made in the interests of reform. It came suddenly, secretly, and without evidence of preparatory investigations or the consideration of alternative nominees. The real purpose of the Schweiker selection was to aid Reagan in winning the presidential nomination, not to promote convention rationality. With Ford approaching a delegate majority, Reagan needed to win new support. By selecting a liberal senator from a large northeastern state, he hoped to gain a last-minute victory. Reagan's act was a traditional attempt to conclude a deal and balance the ticket. It was innovative only in its timing, before the convention, rather than in the bargaining sessions of the convention itself.

In the end, the attempt delayed, but did not prevent, Ford's victory. By selecting a liberal, Reagan damaged his conservative credentials in a party that increasingly placed ideological purity above pragmatic considerations of electoral success. Some critical conservative votes were lost when the Californian acted contrary to his credo, reiterated only two weeks before the Schweiker designation: "I don't believe in the old tradition of picking someone at the opposite end of the political spectrum because he can get some votes you can't get yourself." [40] Reagan also gained a few votes by his bold tactic, but failed to crack the large northeastern delegations; the net effect of his effort was probably to the President's advantage.

Yet Ford, too, was required to depart from past practice in the choice of a running mate. Broad hints of the President's preference were dropped, with considerable attention given to John Connally, who dropped his previous neutrality to endorse the President. A poll was conducted of all convention delegates and alternates, and of all major Republican officeholders and party officials. A long investigative process was launched into the qualifications of nineteen prospective nominees, with intensive attention given to a short list of five possibilities.

The final choice was made only after an all-night session following Ford's own victory. To placate the conservative forces, Reagan was given a virtual veto over the designation,[41] and the most conservative of the remaining candidates was chosen. In the final selection, the President reverted to traditional procedures and traditional ticket-balancing, selecting Senator Robert Dole of Kansas. Moreover, the President then indicated that he was favorable to the future use of the Reagan procedure, the early designation of the running mate. As was true of much of the Republican convention, the Reagan faction appeared to win everything but the presidential nomination.

These changes in the vice-presidential nomination are not certain to be repeated in the future. Carter's deliberate search was permitted only by his own early victory; other candidates may not enjoy the luxury of time. Reagan's early selection of Schweiker was made for the same reasons of political expediency that have operated in the past, and his failure to achieve victory will not encourage others to imitate his example. These innovations will become permanent only if required by law or urged by political necessity. In such circumstances, the 1976 events will provide useful precedents.

After 1976: The Meaning of the Nominations

Each party convention affects the future course of American politics, some profoundly, some minimally. Even with our limited present perspective, it seems likely that the parties' decisions in 1976 will have significant long-term effects.

In both parties, power was shifting to new areas, new leaders, new constituencies. A national population and power shift became evident in the critical role of the southern and Sun Belt states. Reagan's challenge was founded on the increased proportion of delegates allocated to these areas. For Carter, the South provided the vital regional base for an eventual sweeping victory. In the latter case, new rules of proportional representation further underlined the decline of the older areas of power.[42]

Individuals personalized the passing of power in the Democrats. Humphrey and McGovern were given enthusiastic receptions, but their status was that of retiring party elders, comparable in influence to the deceased Democratic Presidents who were present only in honored memory. Two younger men, George Wallace and Edward Kennedy, had greatly affected recent conventions. In 1976, they were literally unheard—Kennedy because he declined an invitation to give a minor speech, Wallace because the public address system failed to amplify the "message" he had delivered for twelve years and that had now fallen on deaf ears.

Attention was reserved for new leaders: a black congresswoman from Texas, Barbara Jordan; the widow and father of the leader of civil disobedience, Martin Luther King, Jr.; the first veteran of the Korean war to be nominated for national office, Walter Mondale; and the southern leader of a new party coalition, Jimmy Carter.

As these individuals exemplify, new groups had come to power in the Democratic party. Blacks were critical, for only they could provide the stamp of legitimacy on a candidate and his views on civil rights, particularly a white man from the Deep South. Women activists, too, needed to be conciliated by offices such as convention chairwoman, by platform pledges, and by promises of equitable representation. Labor, a mainstay of the party in the past, remained, but changed. Major influence was held not by the established leadership of the AFL–CIO but by a coalition of nine unions, including such organizations as the United Automobile Workers and the National Education Association.[43]

These shifts within the party took place even as there was some decline in the visible presence of women, blacks, and young people. More important than a quota for these groups was the reality of their power. The platform, the officers, and the attention of the convention reflected the concerns of such interests as women and blacks better than the symbolism of numerical representation. Thus, blacks themselves concluded that they "have made a significant impact on Democratic Party affairs and have realized many of their long-sought-after goals." [44]

With new politics came new issues. The platform barely mentioned the divisive conflicts of the previous decade—Vietnam, civil disorder, life styles. Contrary to past patterns, the Democrats devoted very little attention to criticism of the Republican administration and instead emphasized a series of proposals for future action. Moderation of past controversies was evidenced by the party's positions on busing, abortion, amnesty for Vietnam war resisters, and the equal rights amendment. The stress of the party program was on economic and social issues.[45]

As divisive issues receded, the Democrats were able to achieve a remarkable unity. The possibility for future conflict remained, as indicated by low-level disputes on rules for future party meetings. The convention was closely divided on a minority report that would mandate a mid-term 1978 party conference of 2,000 delegates, with at least two-thirds elected locally and with a prescribed agenda including discussion of policy issues. This proposal received a narrow plurality of votes but failed of passage because absences resulted in lack of the required absolute majority. The split may presage future conflict in the party at a time when unity is less imperative.

For 1976, at least, unity and change were evident. On the last night of the convention, the barons of the party paid homage to Carter, the new chieftain. Remarkably, a southerner had been nominated, with considerable black support, on a platform endorsing civil rights. The party had been united, in its ticket and program, after a decade of internal strife. The unity, and the transformation, were dramatically symbolized in the last moment of the convention, when the delegates joined in singing "We Shall Overcome." This hymn of civil rights protest had become an anthem for whites and blacks, northerners and southerners. The protestors were now pacified, their dissent now party principle.

Change was personified in the Republican party as well. The GOP's only living former President, Richard Nixon, was not mentioned at the convention. An Arizona congressman presided over its deliberations, and special attention was paid to the view of the Mississippi state chairman, the governor of South Carolina, and a North Carolina senator. Gerald Ford could not win nomination until his conservative credentials were certified by Barry Goldwater, once ostracized as an extremist, and by John Connally, a former Democrat. A contrast in power was presented by Nelson Rockefeller, once able to dictate changes in the party platform, once the most powerful state governor, four times a possible presidential nominee, but now barely able to control his home state, ignored by the delegates, unable to achieve consideration even for renomination as vice-president.

In its platform, the Republican party altered traditional styles but not established policies. Although the incumbent party, relatively little attention was devoted to a defense of the past administration. The emphasis, rather, was an offensive against the Democrats, their new candidate, and their congressional leadership. Traditional values were proclaimed, with the exception of support for the equal rights amendment. Established party doctrines, including a large military budget and economic reliance on private spending, were reemphasized. Only symbolic issues of foreign policy threatened the ideological coherence of the party, but this threat disappeared when the Ford faction accepted the conservatives' rhetorical defense of "morality in foreign policy."

By the last night of the convention, the Republicans too had achieved a large measure of apparent unity. The selection of Senator Dole satisfied most groups other than the extreme conservatives. Ronald Reagan appeared on the platform at the last moment to offer his blessings on the platform and thereby indirectly to the national ticket. The President's acceptance speech, a concentrated attack on the Democrats, provided a standard for the party rally. As the delegates again sang "God Bless America," the repeated theme song of the convention, they could believe that a Republican victory was essential to the continued favor of Providence on their land.

In the longer perspective, the nominations of 1976 were part of a continuing trend toward the decline of the conventions as significant political bodies. No convention since 1952 has taken more than a single ballot to nominate its presidential candidate. Throughout this period, moreover, with the single exception of Ford, the winner of the nomination has been determined before the convention actually convened. Carter's ability to win an overwhelming first-ballot victory, despite the new Democratic rules, is particularly strong testament to the obsolescence of the traditional convention as a place where nominations are decided through the bargaining of party power brokers.

There are many reasons for this trend, and their effects are likely to continue in the future. The critical agencies in presidential nominations have changed. One of the most vital is the mass media, which appraise candidates, evaluate their abilities, and judge their chances of success. The standing of candidates is now certified not by state party leaders but by small, groups of reporters and commentators. "They are acknowledged experts, well connected in political circles throughout the land. Their reports appear in the nation's most prestigious newspapers and respected news broadcasts. . . . Collectively they are what columnist Russell Baker has called 'the Great Mentioniser,' the source of self-fulfilling stories that a person has been 'mentioned' as a possible presidential nominee." [46] The media, particularly television, exaggerate the importance of particular events, bringing candidates quickly to the fore on the basis of a single test. Since their interpretation of these events defines political reality, the New Hampshire primary can be transformed from a minor test of popularity in a minor state to the event that gives a candidate "momentum." By labeling a candidate a "front-runner," they indeed give him a lead; by declaring him the likely winner, they make likely his preconvention victory.[47]

Other factors also tend to the nationalization of politics and consequently to the decline of the conventions. New federal laws on political finance enable candidates to wage independent campaigns without party assistance. State primary laws rob the established organizations of their former control over the choice of delegates. The new essential tools of campaigning, opinion polls and media advertising, are hardly understood by professional politicians and are left to hired hands outside their control. Voter disdain for party labels and the consequent growth of political independence increases the chances of candidates who run in opposition to the party leaders rather than courting their support. The party conventions once were a quadrennial meeting place for the party barons, where they anointed a weak and temporary king. But, as feudalism gave way to the national state, the decentralized American parties are being transformed into national institutions.

The consolidation of the parties is still incomplete and uneven, and has indeed taken different forms among Republicans and Democrats. The Republicans are united ideologically, as evidenced in the lack of substantive differences between Ford and Reagan, in the absence of overt platform conflict in 1976, and in the conservative ideology prevalent among the delegates. They lack organizational coherence, for the GOP, as shown by the 1976 experience, is still a collection of state parties without the discipline to unify behind an obvious leader. The presidential nomination was not the acclamation of an incumbent chief executive. It was the result of wheedling with individual delegates, bargaining over the vice-presidency, and the painfully slow accumulation of a majority.

The Democrats present virtually a reverse image. The party is still not fully unified ideologically, despite the record of 1976. Potential differences remain on issues of race, life style, and foreign policy. Nevertheless, the party has achieved a noticeable degree of organizational coherence, creating national institutions and enforceable rules, and may soon follow with a national definition of party membership and a supportive financial structure of individual dues.

Truly national parties—"able to bring forth programs to which they commit themselves, and with sufficient internal cohesion to carry out these programs" [48]—require both ideological and organizational unity. Each of the parties has moved toward achieving half this goal. Their movement is slow, unsteady, subject to change—but still discernible. In the future this trend may prove to be the most enduring and significant result of the remarkable nominations of 1976.

Issues in the 1976 Presidential Campaign
Henry A. Plotkin

THE main issues of the 1976 campaign emerged in the course of a series of grueling primaries and an extremely close presidential election. The two major political parties had to contend with an electorate traumatized by the war in Vietnam and the repercussions of Watergate and suffering the effects of a deep economic recession. It was crucial, too, that the parties nominate candidates who would respond effectively to the public's increased mistrust of government. Headlines during the election campaign reported growing national scandals involving the CIA and the FBI. At the same time they described an economy that was clearly in the doldrums. It was not surprising that questions involving morality in politics would be stressed along with the more traditional issue of economic prosperity.

The 1976 campaign was one in which the issue positions of both major parties represented a return to normalcy. The stances of both parties on the principal issues reflected their traditional political and economic philosophies. This was in marked contrast to the primary campaigns in which Washington "politics as usual" were challenged by the former governor of California, Ronald Reagan, and by the former governor of Georgia, Jimmy Carter.

In the general election, while the issue of trust in government persisted, candidates returned to traditional debates over federal public policy. To be sure, no candidate was against full employment, cheap energy, strong national defense, the maintenance of civil liberties, or a reduction in the crime rate. Indeed, by 1976, even the most conservative candidate accepted the major premises of Roosevelt's "welfare state." The problem was not whether to carry out these programs, but how much should be spent and from what point they should be administered—not questions designed to excite political passions.

The themes that ran through the election campaign involved the most effective way to solve contemporary problems, especially those relating to the economy. On this question, party differences were clear. Although media pundits would frequently talk about the lack of issues in the campaign, what they failed to see was that both candidates were operating within the limitations imposed by American liberal individualism. Party differences *were palpable* even though they did not reflect fundamental ideological cleavages. Both parties worked within the framework of American welfare-state liberalism; this produced few surprises, but substantial differences remained.

As striking as the differences that emerged between the parties, there were other issues seldom discussed. Women's rights, the urban crises, and the right to dissent—issues so much a part of the politics of the last decade—were largely ignored. The war in Vietnam was not a major issue for the first time in three elections. The nation was forced to confront the question of foreign policy in an age in which OPEC and détente seemed to predominate. Interestingly, these two questions are reminiscent of an older politics in which issues of American autonomy and relations to the Soviet Union were central. With Vietnam no longer an issue, foreign policy would once again focus on the more traditional issues of prosperity at home and peace abroad. Issues concerning life styles also faded from the political scene. No longer did questions about hair length, marijuana, and the counterculture exercise the passions of the public. America seemed to have turned away from many of the abstract issues of the past in order to confront the realities of the present. Traditional issues—employment, taxation, and inflation—dominated the campaign.

The Economy

The deep recession of 1973–74 created shock waves throughout the United States. Rampant inflation eroded incomes while an escalating rate of unemployment swelled the relief rolls. The Amer-

ican people were experiencing a new phenomenon: high inflation and high unemployment. For the middle class, this experience was a profound one. It was to this issue that both national
parties had to respond.

THE REPUBLICANS

The response of the Republican platform to the question of jobs
and inflation was blunt and clear.

> We believe it is of paramount importance that the American people
> understand that the number one destroyer of jobs is inflation. We
> wish to stress that the number one cause of inflation is the govern-
> ment's expansion of the nation's supply of money and credit needed
> to pay for deficit spending. It is above all else deficit spending by
> the federal government which erodes the purchasing power of the
> dollar.[1]

Thus, the way to deal with high unemployment, according to the
Republicans, was to reduce the federal budget. Economy in government became the key to any program that would guarantee a
high rate of employment. Once this was accomplished, it would
become possible for business to expand and create more jobs. The
problem with inflation was that it *discouraged* savings and *encouraged* borrowing. This expansion of private debt made it difficult for business to engage in capital formation, which is the necessary precursor to corporate expansion. The Republicans argued that
the lack of an incentive to save and invest destroyed the mainspring
of capital formation. Reduced capital expenditures meant a lower
rate of productivity and, consequently, fewer jobs.

The Republican platform stressed the negative role that the government plays in stimulating employment. For the Republicans, the
chief enemy was the "spendthrift" Democratic Congress, which
refused to understand that increased spending can lead only to
fiscal disaster. Only by severely limiting the government's fiscal role
could the nation ever hope to escape the scourge of high unemployment. The Democrats, it was argued, fundamentally misun-
derstood the ways that government spending had been responsible
for the nation's economic plight.

> . . . no government can ever add real wealth [purchasing power] to
> an economy by simply turning on the printing presses or by creating

credit out of thin air. All government can do is confiscate and redistribute wealth. No nation can spend its way into prosperity: a nation can only spend its way into bankruptcy.[2]

The position of President Ford and the Republican party on the economy was consonant with the traditional view that the Republicans have always taken. This view is fundamentally antistatist: a disinclination to use state power to solve broad economic questions. The Republican party platform quoted with great approval the remarks of one of its delegates who said she was a Republican because

> Republicans understand the place of government in the people's lives better than the Democrats. Republicans try to find ways to take care of needs through the private sector first while it seems automatic for Democrats to take care of them through the governmental system.[3]

Perhaps no issue was more salient to the Republicans in 1976 than a reliance on the private sector to resolve economic problems. The Republicans obviously were not seeking a return to laissez-faire capitalism, but they argued that "bureaucratic overregulation" by the federal government inhibited the equitable workings of the competitive marketplace. And while the Republican platform was for antitrust laws to help maintain "fair competition in the marketplace,"[4] there was no desire to have the state change the structure of that marketplace. The major issue for the Republicans was limiting the role of government; it was not applying antitrust laws to oligopolistic corporations.

President Ford stressed this theme during his first debate with Jimmy Carter. Ford asserted:

> . . . Carter has endorsed the Democratic platform which calls for more spending, bigger deficits, more inflation and more taxes. . . . Carter in his acceptance speech called for more and more programs which means more and more government.[5]

Ford's position on the issue of government spending called for "less," not "more." According to the President, business was not responsible for the current economic slump. The real villain was the federal government, whose fiscal policies were controlled by the Democratic Congress.

The major issue of President Ford's campaign was a reduction in federal spending, not regulations on business. It was a clear call for placing the burden of employment on the private sector. Government's primary role was to maintain low interest rates and curb its spending. There was no desire to overturn the welfare state, but there was no inclination to expand it either.

THE DEMOCRATS

If the Democratic party has traditionally had one issue most associated with it, that issue is employment. The political coalition formed during the administration of Franklin Roosevelt had as its main source of strength the working people. The Democratic commitment to the needs and aspirations of the poor and laboring classes has been its greatest power at the polls. In 1972, when the McGovernites seemed little concerned with the plight of labor, the Democrats paid a heavy price in election results. The Democrats in 1976 were determined to win back their traditional labor support by taking on the economic policies of the Nixon and Ford administrations.

> The Ford Administration and its economic advisors have been consistently wrong about the sources and cures of the inflation that has plagued our nation and our people. Fighting inflation by curtailing production and increasing unemployment has done nothing to restrain it. With the current level of capacity utilization, we can increase production and employment without rekindling inflation.[6]

Unemployment will not cure inflation, the Democrats argued; rather, the reverse is true. The basic economic assumption made by the Democrats is that increased employment will increase demand, which will lead to corporate expansion to meet that demand. The way to reduce inflation—and ultimately reduce federal spending—is to put people back to work. In fiscal 1976 expenditures and lost revenues due to unemployment cost federal and local governments $103 billion. Indeed, the Democrats argued in their platform that Republican economic policies "have substituted welfare for work." [7] For each percent of the population out of work, $3 billion is spent on unemployment compensation and $2 billion is spent on welfare and related costs. At the same time $14 billion in potential taxes is lost. Full employment must become the major goal of the federal government.[8]

The Democratic platform was quite explicit on the issue of employment. It is the responsibility of the federal government to assist in assuring a full-employment economy:

> The Democratic Party is committed to the *right* of all adult Americans willing, able and seeking work to have opportunities for useful jobs, at living wages. To make that commitment meaningful, we pledge ourselves to the support of legislation that will make every responsible effort to reduce adult unemployment to 3 percent within 4 years.[9]

Jimmy Carter, who was reluctant to support so bold a promise prior to his nomination, eventually came out in favor of the Humphrey-Hawkins full-employment bill. This bill would have actively involved the federal government in guaranteeing the right to a job. The government would, in effect, have become the employer of last resort. There was little inhibition in the Democratic platform about using state power to guarantee their employment goal. They asserted that "at times, direct government involvement in wage and price decisions may be required to insure price stability." [10]

The advocacy of wage and price controls to curb inflation was in sharp contrast to the Republican party position on this issue, which clearly stated that "wage and price controls are not the solution to inflation." [11] The Republicans argued that wage and price controls have proven to be a "dismal failure" that in the long run serve to create "shortages, black markets and higher prices." [12] The Democrats, on the other hand, would utilize state power to reduce the unemployment rate. In fact, in the first debate with Ford, Carter called for the reestablishment of the Civilian Conservation Corps, which had been developed during the New Deal to reduce unemployment: ". . . a CCC-type program would be appropriate to channel money into sharing with the private sector and also local and state governments to employ young people who are now out of work." [13]

PARTY DIFFERENCES

The positions of the two parties on the issue of the economy were quite distinct. The Republican position represented the "trickle-down" theory of economic growth, which means that by expanding corporate investment possibilities, more jobs will eventually be created. The Democratic stance involved a "trickle-up" theory, which argued that by guaranteeing high employment, increased demand would permit business expansion and economic growth.

These two positions reflect traditional differences between our two parties. In the presidential debates, printed literature, and numerous campaign speeches, both Ford and Carter stressed these respective themes.

Indeed, on economic issues the difference between the candidates showed most clearly. Carter, in the two debates on domestic questions, consistently stressed that the federal government must take a more activist role. And while both Carter and Ford held up the vision of ending deficit spending and achieving full employment, their approaches were radically different. They represented two distinct philosophies of state and economic relations and offered the voters a genuine choice of alternatives.

An area in which this issue distinction was highly manifest was tax reform. President Ford and the Republican platform stressed the need for tax policies that will

> hasten capital recovery through a new system of accelerated depreciation, removing the tax burden of equity financing to encourage more capital investment, ending the unfair double taxation of dividends. . . .[14]

This tax formula had as its intent making more available investment capital for the private sector. Again the major theme for the Republicans was the expansion of the private sector in order to increase the rate of economic growth. Once the gross national product began to increase, an upsurge in employment would follow, and if the spending line was held, a net reduction in the federal budget as a percentage of the GNP would occur.

Ford also emphasized the need to alter the tax structure to meet the demands of an increasingly militant middle class. It was essential for the Republican party to offer direct tax relief to middle-class families, who felt squeezed by a government that spent too much on welfare programs for the poor. Much of the taxpaying public's discontent with the government now revolved around a growing sense of being ignored by politicians. If the 1960s were a time when "the other America" was a national priority, the 1970s saw a harassed middle class that would make a claim on the national government. Hence, Ford would argue for the need to reduce taxes for a middle class seemingly fed up with the favored treatment given to the poor.

The Republican tax program asked for a general tax cut to aid working people, "tax credits for college tuition, post secondary technical training and child care payments incurred by working parents." [15] This program was designed to appeal to families that sought a measure of relief from the soaring cost of social services. In order to assist middle-income families, Ford urged that the personal exemption be raised from $750 to $1,000.[16] Again the President asserted that the precondition for tax relief was a sharply reduced federal budget. Ford said in the first campaign debate: "We have to hold the lid on Federal spending; that for every dollar of tax reduction we had to have an equal reduction in Federal expenditures—a one for one proposition." [17]

The Democratic position on taxes reflected a different orientation. Carter considered a major overhaul of the tax system to be the first step toward economic justice. While the Democrats pledged themselves to assist in capital formation, their main emphasis was on the elimination of "inequities" in the tax structure. This would involve closing tax loopholes, ending tax shelters, and striving for a more equitable distribution of income through tax policies. The targets of Carter and the Democrats were the rich, whom they said have not paid their fair share of taxes. Both individual men of wealth and corporations bore the brunt of Carter's criticism during the campaign. He consistently called the tax structure "a disgrace" and emphasized the need for total reform that would lead to an equitable distribution of the society's resources.

> The present tax structure is a disgrace to this country. It is just a welfare program for the rich. As a matter of fact 25 per cent of the total tax deductions go for one per cent of the richest people in this country, and over 50 per cent of the tax credits go for the 14 per cent of the richest people in this country.[18]

Both Ford and Carter strongly argued for tax relief for the middle class, yet what separated them was their strategy to accomplish this task. Ford wanted a reduction in state expenditures; Carter cited the unfairness of the tax system in relation to private wealth. This distinction represented a fundamental difference between the two candidates. It is also indicative of the historical difference between the Republican and Democratic parties. On perhaps no other set of issues in the campaign is this difference more obvious than on economic policy. Inflation, unemployment, and tax policy were the centerpieces of the 1976 campaign. Short-term factors might dominate the headlines, but economics remained a salient issue in the minds of the electorate. And on this issue both candidates were direct about the programs they supported, programs that were greatly at odds with one another.

Although differences on the economy between the candidates became quite clear, their differences on other issues were less certain. This is probably attributable to the fact that a return to political "normalcy" by the two parties was easiest to assess in terms of economic policy. Many other issues of the campaign simply did not lend themselves to the broad analysis that the economy did. Frequently these other issues involved questions of private morality, which American politicians prefer to avoid, or questions that were too complex to be easily explained. Yet the candidates' views on energy, welfare, abortion, the environment, busing, and foreign affairs were substantially different. Campaign analysts were fond of debunking the candidates' stands on these issues as too "vague," or "muddled." It is arguable that what these analysts objected to was not "vagueness" but rather the fact that neither candidate took an extreme position on these questions. In spite of this lack of extremism, the candidates were clear, and their disagreements were significant. But moderation on many issues deprived media interpreters of an opportunity simply to relegate the candidates' views into dichotomous categories. It was popular to accuse both Ford and Carter of "waffling" on issues. Although an occasional reversal did occur, both the candidates and their platforms served to clarify more than confuse important national issues.

The Social Issues

Some policy questions in the 1976 campaign concerned the "social issues." A diverse group, these issues had the common characteristic of being related to the disturbing effects of social change. They included emotional questions of race relations, matters of individual morality and conscience, and reform of the welfare system.

RACE RELATIONS
The social issue that had gripped the nation over the last two decades was race relations. From the time of the *Brown* vs. *Board of Education* Supreme Court decision, the question of racial equality has been at the center of American national politics. The sit-ins in

the South, the landmark legislation of the Johnson years, and the gradual desegregation of southern schools marked substantial progress on this issue.

The urban riots of the 1960s, the growth of militant black ideologies, and the tragic assassination of Martin Luther King, Jr., amply demonstrated that progress in race relations does not come without great cost. Still, in 1976 there was a different quality to the debate over race relations. The battle for legal and political equality, in a formal sense at least, had been won. The major race issue in 1976 was to what extent the Supreme Court's ruling on school busing would be enforced. The issue represented more than school integration; it symbolized for blacks whether the federal government would support genuine integration or would remain content with the mere appearance of equality.

A profound revolution had occurred in America in the past twenty years. It had forced whites to adapt to the reality of a substantial black presence in the nation. Despite this adaptation, a backlash had also clearly begun, corresponding to the soaring urban crime rate, the mounting cost of welfare, and the fears about school busing. This backlash did not infer that white Americans were prepared to return to a more primitive mode of race relations, but it did signal to the parties and their candidates that it was time to slow down the thrust toward full integration in order to avoid further violence. This was evident not only in Boston, but also in dozens of other cities across the country.

Both President Ford and Governor Carter took clear positions against the mandatory busing of schoolchildren. Carter asserted that the "only kids who get bused are poor children," [19] and Ford said that court-ordered busing was not "the right way to get quality education." [20] Carter, specifically, backed a plan calling for the voluntary busing of schoolchildren that would ameliorate the problem of segregated housing patterns created by segregated school systems. Ford agreed with Carter about the importance of maintaining stable neighborhoods and argued against federal housing acts that would destroy homogeneous neighborhoods.

Perhaps the main distinction between the candidates on the issue of integrated schools was Ford's advocacy of a constitutional amendment banning busing unless Congress acted to protect the concept of neighborhood schools. "If Congress continues to fail to act," the Republican platform warned, "we would favor consideration of an amendment to the Constitution forbidding the assignment of children to schools on the basis of race." [21]

The Democrats were clearly against a constitutional amendment to stop school busing. Yet their overall position on busing was obviously tempered by the need to appeal to urban ethnics, who were up in arms over the prospect of mandatory busing. Hence the Democrats and their candidate talked mainly about the need to improve the quality of education and saw busing as "a judicial tool of last resort for the purpose of achieving school desegregation." [22]

Neither candidate wanted the issue of busing to be a major one. Indeed, most political candidates prefer, to the extent possible, to evade such questions because of the very real likelihood of offending passionate minorities for whom that one issue is all that really counts in the election.

THE MORAL QUESTIONS

Of all the social issues raised in the 1976 campaign, the one that was most uncomfortable for both Carter and Ford was abortion. The rise of the women's movement in the 1960s, along with the general loosening of sexual mores, had made "abortion on demand" a rallying cry for the politically liberal and the sexually liberated. With the passage of liberal abortion laws in such states as New York, the guilt and shame previously associated with abortion began to fade. The once overwhelming power of the Catholic church on this issue had been severely eroded by the continued secularization of American politics with its emphasis on personal liberty and freedom of choice.

Yet, in the mid-1970s forces began to emerge that would ask public authorities to reevaluate their stand on certain questions. The specific impetus for the extension of this thrust to a national platform was the 1973 Supreme Court decision that allowed abortions within the first three months of pregnancy. Right-to-life movements began to erode the gains made by pro-abortionists and asked that the abortion question be made part of the national political agenda. The debate on abortion, especially in the person of Right-to-Life presidential candidate Ellen McCormack, became a national issue, forcing Carter and Ford to take positions on it.

A fundamental precept of American politics is that presidential candidates are to be conservative on moral questions. Present and future Presidents must and will offer obeisance to the strictures of traditional morality and not be seen as "soft" on questions involving divorce, atheism, or adultery. Hence it was no great surprise that both Carter and Ford were personally opposed to abortion. The only real difference between them was that Ford supported the idea of a constitutional amendment that would grant each state the right to set its own standards governing abortion. Carter opposed such an amendment (winning the enmity of many Catholic prelates), but he also opposed the use of federal funds to pay for abortions.

Among the more pressing issues in the 1976 campaign was welfare reform. Financial crises in New York and other major cities brought to national attention the economic burden that welfare payments placed on them. The need for a broad federal initiative to deal with this issue was of central importance for Jimmy Carter and the Democratic party.

> We should move toward replacement of our existing inadequate and wasteful system with a simplified system of income maintenance, substantially financed by the federal government.[23]

This program involved more than the federalization of welfare; it also called for "an income floor both for the working poor and the poor not in the labor market." [24] This is a clear extension of welfare-state economics toward the establishment of a guaranteed income. The level of funding for this program may not be high, but it does represent a commitment for the assumption of welfare responsibility by the federal government.

> The patchwork of federal, state and local programs encourages unfair variations in benefit levels among the states and benefits in many states are below the standards for even lowest-income budgets.[25]

The position of President Ford and the Republicans on the question of welfare was at odds with that of the Democrats. While Ford stressed the inequities of the present system, he did not propose an alternative. Instead, the general thrust of the Republicans was to reduce welfare cheating, access to food stamps, and, in general, to attack the Democratic Congress that had produced "a jumble of degrading, dehumanizing, wasteful, overlapping and inefficient programs." [26] The key to the Republican position was to assist the "deserving poor" and to assume that any American who wanted to work would find a job as the economic picture improved. Indeed, the solution to welfare problems is a growth economy, and toward that task the Republicans dedicated themselves. They emphatically rejected the concept of a guaranteed income because it would reduce the work incentive.

Energy and the Environment

Energy is an issue of great national concern. The Arab oil boycott along with the dire predictions by environmentalists about the shrinking supply of available energy has compelled the American public to acknowledge the necessity of a rational energy policy. The United States historically has been a nation where the bounty of nature has precluded the necessity of confronting a scarcity of natural resources. Today, however, there is a growing awareness that consumption patterns must somehow be altered to adapt to a clearly changed energy situation. The public also may now understand the complex relationship between domestic energy consumption and a growing dependence on foreign powers.

The energy issue is closely tied to questions about the preservation of the environment. Like energy, environmental concerns (as distinguished from simple conservation) are fairly new items on the national agenda. Earlier perceptions by the public of an unlimited nature have been dashed by polluted cities, fouled lakes and streams, and the threat of industrial expansion into the natural wilderness. The decisions facing the candidates in 1976 concerned the sacrifices they were willing to ask of the American people. What policies should the two major parties advocate to deal with questions of energy and the environment?

On this issue, differences between the two major candidates were clear and consonant with broader philosophical distinctions between their two parties. Ford was committed to a policy of economic growth, which required cheap energy. He had vetoed bills concerning strip mining, federal land-use planning, and others that would increase the federal government's involvement in establishing more standards regarding pollution. The major tradeoff the President had been willing to make was that of economic expansion for environmental regulation. This position was a logical outgrowth of Ford's commitment to assist the growth of the private sector, which, consequently, would provide more jobs.[27]

Ford also advocated an "accelerated" use of nuclear energy as a way of decreasing America's dependency on foreign oil. This position was strenuously opposed by environmentalists, who argued that the potential for disaster in the use of nuclear reactors far outweighed the potential benefits. The Republicans justified the use of nuclear reactors in terms of easing the cost of energy, which would help to stimulate industrial expansion.[28]

Jimmy Carter took a much different position on questions of the environment and energy. He made it clear that in any conflict between the environment and industrial expansion, he would sacrifice industrial expansion. The Democratic platform argued that this was essentially a bogus choice, for ". . . environmental protection creates jobs. . . . The Democratic Party believes that a concern for the environment need not and must not stand in the way of a much-needed policy of high economic growth." [29]

The major distinction between the two candidates was Carter's reliance on the federal government in long-range land-use planning. The Democrats do not accept the Republican premise that jobs will be lost if too much federal regulation of the environment takes place, so they were able to argue with equal vigor for both economic expansion and environmental control. The Democrats were also not hesitant about increasing the role of the national government in pursuit of their ends, nor were they hesitant about asking the private sector to share the economic burden.

On the question of energy, the Democrats argued for strong federal rule in the regulation and development of the nation's energy future. They directly attacked the role played by the private sector:

> The time has come to deal with the realities of the energy crises, not its illusions. The realities are that rising energy prices, falling domestic supply, increasing demand, and the threat to national security of growing imports, have not been contained by the private sector.[30]

Again, the major thrust of the Democrats was away from reliance on the mechanisms of the marketplace. This was in sharp contrast to the Republicans, who consistently argued for a reliance on market mechanisms that included allowing the price of energy to fluctuate with demand. The Democrats and Carter questioned this policy and called on the federal government to establish more controls on energy including the assurance that competition will be maintained in the oil industry.[31] The threat of divestiture of the oil industry was a significant part of their criticism of the private sector's handling of the energy question.

> We support the legal prohibition against corporate ownership of competing types of energy. We believe such "horizontal" concentration of economic power to be dangerous, both to the national interest and to the functioning of the competitive system.[32]

Carter also strongly disagreed with Ford's position on nuclear energy. He argued that dependence on nuclear power should be kept to a minimum. Carter's position on this issue was clear and concise, as would be expected from someone with his experience in the field. He argued that the energy needs of the nation would be better served by an increased use of coal instead of by nuclear reactors. The development of a sophisticated coal technology would allow many industries at present dependent on oil and natural gas to convert to coal. This policy would also assist the railroads because a rail network would be essential to transport the coal. Too, a greater reliance on coal would stimulate the economy of areas such as Appalachia, which have become poverty belts because of the increased use of oil and natural gas.

Foreign Policy and Defense

The future course of American foreign policy came under great scrutiny in the 1976 campaign. Détente, the Strategic Arms Limitation Talks (SALT), the Middle East, southern Africa, China, and a host of other issues were debated during the primaries and in the general election campaigns. Foreign policy was thought to be the Republican's strongest issue. The Nixon and Ford administrations were responsible for opening up relations with the People's Republic of China, easing tensions with the Soviet Union, maintaining peace in the Middle East, and most important, avoiding any situation that might cost American lives. Ford continually stressed the theme that America was at peace; and after the traumatic experience of Vietnam, the nation was clearly not in the mood for any further foreign adventures.

Yet, despite these accomplishments, there was a sense of disquiet about international affairs. Had the United States given away too much at SALT? What were the nature and extent of U.S. clandestine activities in Chile? Was there too much secrecy about foreign policy? Would the Arabs attempt another oil boycott? Finally, what had been the role of Henry Kissinger? All these questions would prove to be major issues in the campaign.

SPECIFIC ISSUES

The individual who loomed largest in the campaign—aside from the major candidates—was Henry Kissinger. As he had been for Ronald Reagan, Kissinger became Carter's favorite target. Accusing Kissinger of being a "Lone Ranger," Carter attacked the morality of American foreign policy. He criticized U.S. support for authoritarian regimes in South Korea and Chile. He argued that the defense budget was too large and could be cut by from $5 billion to $7 billion without adversely affecting U.S. security.[33]

While these attacks may seem more than faintly reminiscent of the McGovern position on foreign policy, Carter also attacked from a conservative stance. He criticized Kissinger for giving away too much at SALT, threatened economic warfare on the Arabs if they engaged in another oil boycott, and chided Ford on Eastern Europe. In the second debate with Ford, Carter attacked the Helsinki accords for failing to protect the individual liberties of Eastern Europeans:

> In the case of the Helsinki Agreements, it may have been a good agreement in the beginning but we have failed to enforce the so-called basket three part which insures the right of people to migrate, to join their families, to be free, to speak out.[34]

Carter's position on foreign policy seemed both conservative *and* liberal. His arguments against Helsinki and his skepticism about SALT were examples of conservative positions. His criticism of the morality of American foreign policy with authoritarian regimes was reflective of a liberal stance. In addition, Carter's views on the need for more openness in the foreign policy decision-making process bespoke the liberal's concern with democratic procedural values.

> . . . I would quit conducting the decision-making process in secret, as has been characteristic of Mr. Kissinger and Mr. Ford. In many instances we have made agreements . . . that have been revealed later on to our embarrassment.[35]

Carter's strategy of adopting both left- and right-wing positions on foreign policy left Ford stranded in an uncertain middle.

The middle was uncertain in large part because of the ubiquitous role that Kissinger played in the shaping of American foreign policy. Kissinger's idea of the balance of power was translated into a policy that subordinated most international issues to U.S./USSR relations. This "realistic" approach to foreign policy was predicated on achieving a reasonable balance of military power with the Soviet Union and attempting to find areas of overlapping interest where negotiations could take place. It was also an acknowledgment that there were real disagreements between the two nations and that the goal of each was to minimize them. In addition, Kissinger felt that a relaxation of tensions was needed for both nations to limit their international aspirations. The ultimate hope of Kissinger's policies was to establish a web of interrelationships with the Soviet Union that would make conflict less probable. Hence his emphasis on trade with Russia became a central component of his policy.

While the Democrats were not arguing for a return to the cold war, they were clearly not buying Kissinger's view of "balance of power." Carter talked about "world order politics," which presumably was less Soviet-oriented in its foci and more concerned with Europe and the Third World. This probably meant policies more sensitive to the economic problems of the industrialized world and their relations with underdeveloped countries. It also seemed to recognize that while U.S./Soviet relations were vital, it was also necessary to confront a rapidly changing world economy.

This perspective was never fully defined, but Carter's seeming rejection of Kissinger's views closely corresponded to the public's more general mistrust of Soviet motives. Hence Carter did not reject the idea of SALT; he simply argued that he would be a tougher negotiator. He did not advocate "sweeping back the Red tide in Europe"; he was simply not willing to grant Russia the "moral" right to rule there. He did not object to a strong U.S. leadership role in world politics; he did propose that the United States work more closely with its allies.

The second debate on foreign policy was to open up an unanticipated issue. This had to do with Ford's error on Eastern Europe when he argued that "there is no Soviet domination of Eastern Europe and there never will be under a Ford administration." [36] This blunder was quickly picked up by Carter when he retorted:

"I would like to see Mr. Ford convince the Polish Americans and the Czech Americans and the Hungarian Americans . . . that those countries don't live under the domination and supervision of the Soviet Union behind the Iron Curtain." [37]

This exchange clearly hurt the President. Its effect probably was to make Ford's experience in foreign affairs less of an advantage than it might otherwise have been. It also allowed Carter to make direct appeals to Eastern European ethnics. The question of the role of the Soviets in Eastern Europe was not really a profound one, but it gave Carter an opportunity to question the President's competence in the delicate area of foreign policy. In general, these questions were all subordinate to one major issue: what was the purpose of American foreign policy?

THE AMERICAN PURPOSE

The United States had clearly not articulated a broad purpose for its foreign policy. The truculence of the cold-war years had been tempered by the war in Indochina and led in 1972 to an attempt by the liberal wing of the Democratic party to make America more isolationist.

In the 1972 election Democratic candidate George McGovern had used the slogan "Come Home America" to signify his belief in a reduced American role in international affairs. In 1976 the position of "Come Home America" was largely forgotten, except as an advertisement urging people to buy a Ford automobile. The neo-isolationist position of the McGovernites was advocated by neither Ford nor Carter. Instead, much of the foreign policy debate in 1976 involved a clarification of the purposes that lay behind U.S. participation in world affairs.

For Carter, the major issue was the direction and purpose of U.S. foreign policy. The leitmotif of Carter's campaign was to stress a return of morality and trust in government. In this context, foreign policy was simply another example of the lack of American leadership. In June of 1976, Carter's campaign manager, Hamilton Jordan, asserted:

> We decided we would offer a basic appeal to voters, just like every other candidate. Scoop [Senator Henry Jackson] talked about jobs. Carter talks about trust and his faith that the country is better than it seems to be.[38]

Although Carter openly embraced many of the traditional Democratic party positions on the issues, he clearly based his personal appeal on questions involving morality, leadership, and trust. It is difficult to determine which issues were most salient for the electorate, but, to Carter, the lack of these three characteristics in public men was responsible for the public's feeling of political inefficacy.

Indeed, since the end of the Second World War there has been a sense that the United States has lost its moorings, that somehow the nation has become corrupted not simply by dishonest public officials but also by a lack of moral purpose. Carter's argument for a more open, less secretive government was based on a conception of government contained in John Jay's famous comment, "Here, the people rule." Whether President Carter can fulfill the promise of a government that reflects the decency of its citizens is obviously an open question. It is fair to say that, more than any other modern President, he has committed himself to make palpable that ancient ideal, the "consent of the governed."

The Presidential Election
Gerald M. Pomper

No, 'tis not so deep as a well, nor so wide as a church-door,
but 'tis enough, 'twill serve.
— Shakespeare, *Romeo and Juliet*

ECEIVING a bare majority of the popular vote, gaining a thin margin of the electoral votes, and carrying a minority of the states, Jimmy Carter was elected President of the United States on November 2, 1976.

Carter's victory climaxed an astonishing year in American politics, an appropriate ending to the bicentennial of the nation's revolution. The turmoil of independence declared in 1776 was paralleled by the turmoil of political change evident in 1976. The surprising outcome was the election of a one-term Georgia governor and the first defeat of an incumbent President in forty-four years.

In this chapter, we analyze these results, the campaign which preceded the balloting, and the likely consequences of the election. We begin with the principal choice of the voters, the selection of Jimmy Carter.

The Results

THE GEOGRAPHY OF THE VOTE

A chart of the presidential election results presents a distorted picture. As viewed on a national map, the United States appears virtually divided between two hostile blocs of states. The shaded area,

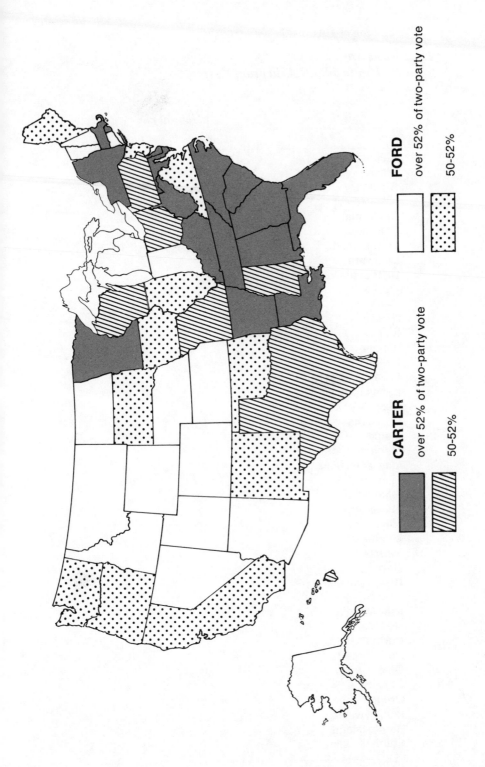

CARTER

over 52% of two-party vote

50-52%

FORD

over 52% of two-party vote

50-52%

Table 3.1

1976 Presidential Election Results _____

State	Electoral vote	
	Carter	Ford
Alabama	9	
Alaska		3
Arizona		6
Arkansas	6	
California		45
Colorado		7
Connecticut		8
Delaware	3	
District of Columbia	3	
Florida	17	
Georgia	12	
Hawaii	4	
Idaho		4
Illinois		26
Indiana		13
Iowa		8
Kansas		7
Kentucky	9	
Louisiana	10	
Maine		4
Maryland	10	
Massachusetts	14	
Michigan		21
Minnesota	10	
Mississippi	7	
Missouri	12	
Montana		4
Nebraska		5
Nevada		3
New Hampshire		4
New Jersey		17
New Mexico		4
New York	41	
North Carolina	13	
North Dakota		3
Ohio	25	
Oklahoma		8
Oregon		6
Pennsylvania	27	
Rhode Island	4	
South Carolina	8	

	Popular vote [a]		Percentage of two-party vote	
	Carter	Ford	Carter	Ford
	659,170	504,070	56.7	43.3
	44,055	71,555	38.1	61.9
	295,602	418,642	41.4	58.6
	498,604	267,903	65.0	35.0
	3,742,284	3,882,244	49.1	50.9
	460,801	584,456	44.1	55.9
	647,895	719,261	47.4	52.6
	122,559	109,780	52.8	47.2
	137,818	27,873	83.2	16.8
	1,636,000	1,469,531	52.7	47.3
	979,427	483,753	66.9	33.1
	147,375	140,003	51.3	48.7
	126,649	204,151	38.3	61.7
	2,271,295	2,364,269	49.0	51.0
	1,014,714	1,185,958	46.1	53.9
	619,931	632,863	49.5	50.5
	430,421	502,752	46.1	53.9
	615,717	531,762	53.7	46.3
	661,365	587,446	53.0	47.0
	232,279	236,320	49.6	50.4
	759,612	672,661	53.0	47.0
	1,429,475	1,030,276	58.1	41.9
	1,696,714	1,893,742	47.3	52.7
	1,070,440	819,395	56.6	43.4
	381,329	366,846	51.0	49.0
	998,387	927,443	51.8	48.2
	149,259	173,703	46.2	53.8
	233,293	359,219	39.4	60.6
	92,479	101,273	47.7	52.3
	147,645	185,935	44.3	55.7
	1,444,653	1,509,588	48.9	51.1
	201,148	211,419	48.8	51.2
	3,389,558	3,100,791	52.2	47.8
	927,365	741,960	55.6	44.4
	136,078	153,470	47.0	53.0
	2,011,621	2,000,505	50.1	49.9
	532,442	545,708	49.4	50.6
	490,350	491,909	49.9	50.1
	2,327,423	2,204,355	51.4	48.6
	227,636	181,249	55.7	44.3
	450,807	346,149	56.6	43.4

Table 3.1 (continued)

State	Electoral vote	
	Carter	Ford
South Dakota		4
Tennessee	10	
Texas	26	
Utah		4
Vermont		3
Virginia		12
Washington		9
West Virginia	6	
Wisconsin	11	
Wyoming		3
Totals	297	241

a Scattered additional votes totaled 745,042 for Eugene McCarthy (1%), 170,673 for Lester Maddox, and 47,790 for others.

SOURCES: *Congressional Quarterly Weekly Report* 34 (6 November 1976): 3118; *New York Times,* 13 December 1976, p. 69.

representing the states carried by Carter, constitutes a virtually contiguous area running from Massachusetts and the Northeast southward to the old Confederacy. There are, to be sure, some isolated bastions of the Democrats in the upper Midwest, and some scattered Republican pockets along the Atlantic coast. Nevertheless, the Republicans appear visually to occupy a different country. This "other nation" has a territorial extension into the midsection of the continent, from Indiana to Iowa, but its core is the solidly loyal states of the Great Plains, the Mountain states, and the Pacific coast.

This portrait of the balloting reflects the character of the Electoral College, in which the states vote as units. All of a state's electoral votes are cast for its leading candidate, however small his popular margin in the entire state. A thin Carter lead in New York still yielded a monolithic bloc of 41 electoral votes; an even thinner Ford edge gained California's 45 ballots. In this decisive tally, Carter won 297 of the total 538 votes, or 55 percent. As is typical of the electoral vote, the winner's margin was exaggerated over his popular vote.[1]

In this count, we do indeed see a geographical concentration.

Popular vote [a]		Percentage of two-party vote	
Carter	Ford	Carter	Ford
147,068	151,505	49.3	50.7
825,879	633,979	56.6	43.4
2,082,319	1,953,294	51.6	48.4
182,110	337,908	35.0	65.0
78,789	100,387	44.0	56.0
813,896	836,554	49.3	50.7
717,323	777,732	48.0	52.0
435,864	314,726	58.1	41.9
1,040,232	1,004,987	50.9	49.1
62,239	92,717	40.2	59.8
40,827,394	39,145,977	51.05	48.95

[handwritten annotations] Diff 1,681,417   50.4% of total vote if he had all other votes right   V = 31   X = 7

Carter's victory was based on the union of his southern base and long-standing Democratic areas in the industrialized Northeast and Midwest. Once past the South and the banks of the Mississippi, Carter could win no state majorities except in the unique islands of Hawaii. Although millions of voters throughout the nation voiced support of the Democratic candidate, they spoke with the distinct accents of the South and East.

This picture of the vote is engaging to the eye, and its symmetry appeals to the intellect. In fact, however, it is an inaccurate portrait. The election of 1976 was a national decision, not a sectional division along a geographical line. The election indeed divided the voters; but they divided within states, not among them. The choice between Carter and Ford did not resolve into one of a solid South opposed to a granite West. The closeness of the national vote was paralleled in most states of the Union.

Nationally, the overall result was 51 percent of the two-party vote for Carter, 49 percent for Ford. (Of the total vote, minor candidates such as Eugene McCarthy and Lester Maddox won only about one of a hundred votes.) As detailed in table 3.1, similar breakdowns were evident from Maine to Hawaii. In only twenty of the fifty states and the District of Columbia were the two contenders more than ten percentage points apart. Indeed, the results could easily have been turned into an electoral landslide for either candidate. A shift of a single percentage point would have added 87 electoral votes to Carter's total, while a two-point change would have given him 440 of the total of 539 electoral votes. In the opposite direction, a change of but one vote in a hundred would have brought the incumbent President to victory by adding 43 electoral votes to his total. A two-point change would have yielded 353 electoral votes and a strong mandate. Eighteen states were in this narrow range.*

The geography of the vote can be considered in another way, by comparing the November records of Carter and Ford to their records in the earlier nominating primaries.** For both candidates, victories in these contests for delegates had been vital in winning their party designations. For the Democratic candidate, there was a clear continuity in his bases of support throughout the political year. The states in which he won the primaries, in the South as well as in Pennsylvania, Wisconsin, and Ohio, also tended to vote for him in November. Conversely, his weakness in the western region, evident in the spring, continued through November. For the President, there was little continuity; he lost a dozen states, particularly in the East and South, that had endorsed him for the party nomination, while he did best in those western states that had earlier supported Ronald Reagan within the Republican party.[2] Carter therefore created a coalition of some durability in his nomination, while Ford's was of limited viability.

THE DEMOGRAPHY OF THE VOTE

Although electoral ballots are cast by states, votes are cast by individual voters, and it is their decisions that ultimately elect the President. Analysis of the 1976 election must therefore focus on these millions of individual decisions.

A division of the electorate by vital demographic groups, as in table 3.2, shows that the most important groups in Carter's victory were racial minorities and union members. The Georgian won five of every six votes cast by blacks; he actually was the minority choice

---

* The standard deviation of the Democratic vote is a statistical measure of the similarity of state results. This statistic in 1976 (6.3%) was lower than in any presidential election since 1844, with the single exception of 1960.

** See chapter 1 for full discussion of the presidential nominations.

Table 3.2
Social Groups and the Presidential Vote, 1972 and 1976
(in percent)

	1972		1976	
	Nixon	*McGovern*	*Ford*	*Carter*
Party				
Republicans	94	6	89	11
Independents	66	34	52	48
Democrats	42	58	20	80
Ideology				
Liberal	31	69	26	74
Moderate	69	31	47	53
Conservative	87	13	70	30
Occupation				
Professional/managerial	68	32	57	43
White collar	63	37	49	51
Blue collar	61	39	41	59
Union Households				
Members	57	43	38	62
Nonmembers	67	33	52	48
Community				
Cities over 500,000	42	58	40	60
Suburbs–small cities	63	37	47	53
Rural: 5,000 and less	71	29	53	47
Religion				
Protestant	69	31	54	46
Catholic	60	40	45	55
Jewish	37	63	32	68
Race				
White	70	30	52	48
Black	13	87	17	83
Other	32	68	18	82
Sex				
Male	68	32	48	52
Female	62	38	48	52
Age				
18–21	46	54	51	49
22–29	55	45	44	56
30–44	66	34	48	52
45–59	68	32	52	48
60 and over	71	29	52	48
Income [a]				
(Under $5,000)				
Under $8,000	57	43	38	62
($5,000–$10,000)				
$8,000–$12,000	62	38	43	57

Table 3.2 (continued)

	1972		1976	
	Nixon	*McGovern*	*Ford*	*Carter*
($10,001–$15,000)				
$12,001–$20,000	67	33	50	50
(Over $15,000)				
Over $20,000	69	31	62	38
Region				
East	59	41	48	52
Midwest	61	39	51	49
South	72	28	46	54
Far West	61	39	53	47

a Figures in parentheses are income categories for 1972.

SOURCES: For 1972, the election survey of the Center for Political Studies, University of Michigan; for 1976, *New York Times*, 4 November 1976, p. 25. In both years regional data are based on the actual vote.

of white Americans. In a close election, any sizable group can claim to be critical, but in 1976 this claim can be most deservedly made by blacks. It is unlikely that Carter would have carried any region, even the South, without black support. Thus, the first true southerner to be elected President since the pre-Civil War period owed his victory to the descendants of the slaves freed in that war. The South, once segregated, had achieved integration in the polling place, and with it the triumph of a native son.

Union members were the other group essential to the Carter victory. A mainstay of the Democratic coalition of the past, the unionized working class had deserted the party frequently in recent national elections, voting for Richard Nixon over George McGovern in 1972. Although Carter was not the favorite candidate of organized labor earlier in the year, he won quick approval from the AFL–CIO after his nomination. The organization then worked vigorously to register union members, campaign among them, and bring them to the polls on Election Day. This effort was successful, stimulating over three of every five unionists to support the Democratic candidate. Democratic victories in such states as Pennsylvania, Ohio, New York, and Wisconsin could be properly attributed to the union campaign.

The labor movement's work was particularly important in 1976 because of the financial limitations placed on candidates and party organizations by the new election finance law. Almost all of the sparse available funds were devoted to the candidates' travel and to the mass media. As a result, there was virtually no money on hand for headquarters, leaflets, or door-to-door canvassing.[3]

The unions, however, were not restricted. Under a Supreme Court ruling made early in the year, organizations could not be restricted in their direct expenditures, only in their contributions to the candidates.[4] The labor movement was free to spend its own funds to register members, distribute campaign literature to them, and bring out the vote. In many states, unions—as well as black organizations—in effect supplanted the traditional role of organized parties. For the Democrats, the happy result was an increased turnout among the working class, which brought the thin but critical margin of victory.

Carter also won pluralities in other social groupings, but his margin was below expectations among Catholics, Jews, young persons, and the white nonunionized working class. All these groups preferred Carter to Ford, but the important fact about the election was that their support was of relatively modest proportions. Catholics, for example, had been a major element in Democratic victories of the past. In this election, too, they voted for the party of Franklin Roosevelt, but by only about a 5–4 margin, significantly below past performance, and in contrast to the normal expectation of a 63 percent Democratic vote.[5] If similar defections had occurred among other groups, Gerald Ford would have been reelected.

To compensate for losses among the traditional loyalists of the Democratic party, Carter was able to win new backing. Even though he did not gain a majority of these groups, he did better than would be expected for a candidate of his party. Compared to Humphrey and McGovern, Carter did quite well among the middle-aged, small-town residents, and whites. Perhaps responding to Carter's own agricultural background, rural residents gave him almost half their vote, bringing the Georgian close to success in many farm states, accounting for the margin of victory in such states as Ohio and Wisconsin, and achieving a close race in New Jersey.

The vote of white Protestants is particularly illustrative of the shifts in the vote. Among this predominant group, Carter won 46 percent, an extraordinary 14-point gain over McGovern's weak performance in 1972. By way of contrast, Carter gained only 8 points over the 1972 Democratic proportion among Catholics and barely improved at all the party's position among Jews. The explanation for these variations surely is to be found in Carter's own religion. His well-publicized Baptist beliefs increased his appeal to coreligionists in the South and among southern migrants to other regions, while restricting his attractiveness somewhat among other religious groups.

The Carter coalition, demographically, is a unique alliance. It is not simply the renewal of the Democratic majorities first assembled by Franklin Roosevelt. Included are some voters from past Democratic groups and some returning defecters, but also some previous opponents of the party. A purely "traditional" vote could not have brought the Democrats victory, for such erstwhile supporters as manual workers are a shrinking proportion of the electorate. Even where a vote appears traditional, moreover, the appearance may be deceptive. Southern support for Carter may seem like a return to the region's historical loyalty to the Democratic party. But the past record of the region was built on the votes of whites alone, who supported the one-party system in order to maintain segregation. The vote for Carter, to the contrary, was a biracial vote for a candidate particularly dependent on blacks and with an integrationist record. His regional victory was not a return to the past, but rather the most dramatic evidence of the transformation of southern politics.[6]

The change in the Democratic party is further seen in the vaunted "big city" vote. Although Carter did well in these areas, his record was scarcely better than that of McGovern in 1972. He could achieve victory only by bringing in new votes from suburbs, small towns, and rural areas. The simple fact is that the large cities no longer carry decisive impact in presidential politics. Their populations have declined, in absolute numbers in some cases, and generally in relation to the rest of the nation. As a result, the famous urban party machines can no longer swing their states' blocs of electoral votes.

This change was vividly illustrated in 1976 by the returns from Chicago, site of the last significant remaining urban machine. The Democratic organization there actually performed quite well in this election, bringing Carter over two-thirds of the Chicago vote, a significantly better performance than in 1960, when the city's 63 percent vote was credited with the election of John Kennedy. But the weight of power had shifted in these years. From over a third of the total state vote in 1960, the city of Chicago had declined to only a quarter of the Illinois electorate in 1976.[7] Suburban areas had become the new locus of power in Illinois, and in the nation. It was their predominant Republican vote that won the state for Gerald Ford, and almost captured the Presidency. Future Democratic candidates will be still more compelled to extend their efforts beyond the cities' boundaries.

The Campaign

The election followed a national campaign remarkable in two very different aspects. The electoral battle was notable in the apparent change it made in the fortunes of the candidates, bringing President Ford from an incredible deficit of 33 percentage points in the opinion surveys to near victory. It was this aspect of the campaign that received the most attention, with observers regarding the Republican effort as brilliant or the Democratic effort as flawed.

The other remarkable aspect of the campaign is of quite a different order. In the most vital sense, what is striking about the 1976 campaign is how *little* importance it had. Those events of the battle that received the greatest attention in September and October finally had no determining influence on the outcome. Reporters and commentators, needing new material for their articles and broadcasts, devoted much attention to the candidates' statements and misstatements, their campaign travels and campaign obstacles, their alliances and conflicts with local organizations. The voters appear to have taken a longer view.

In the end, the outcome was decided by those factors that existed and were in the minds of the electors before the first burst of oratory. These crucial factors were that Jimmy Carter was a Democrat, that Gerald Ford was President, and that the economy was in a period of uncertainty. These dimensions of the electoral decision never changed. Carter was aided by his party label, Ford by his incumbency. The balance between these influences would be tipped by the economy.

The ultimate effect of the campaign was conservative. It restored these basic factors to a central position in the voters' minds. It renewed old allegiances, particularly those of party and class.[8] It again emphasized those qualities of the candidates that had been known and accepted for some time, particularly the solidity of Ford and the novelty of Carter. It underlined the moderate character of the voters' ideological preferences and the dominance of the two-party system. In its total effect, even with some minor variations, the campaign did not change the voters' preferences. Rather, it made the voters conscious of politics, focused their perceptions, and brought them to the polls.

CARTER TAKES THE LEAD

Three distinct phases can be located in the 1976 presidential campaign. The first, extending from the national conventions through the week of Labor Day, was that of Carter's apparent mastery. After the Democratic convention, both the Gallup and Harris polls gave him better than a 2–1 margin over Ford. This gap narrowed considerably, to about ten to twelve percentage points, after the President received the nomination of his party in August. This margin was a more meaningful measure of the race in its early stage. Still, virtually all observers except the most steadfast Republicans were agreed that there would soon be a new resident in the White House. One reference dictionary, about to go to press with a new edition, even included Carter in an appendix listing all the American Presidents. Confident of victory, the Georgian allocated some of his scarce federal campaign funds to planning the next administration.

Even at the time, it was clear that Carter's lead was subject to change. He was a new political personality and therefore likely to win support from a public scarred by the actions of well-known politicians. Because of his quick rise to prominence, his record, character, and policies had not yet received intense scrutiny. Furthermore, because of his easy victory in the Democratic convention, he had a united party behind him, and no unreconciled opponents. Yet, his standing was "soft," as his own advisers admitted. Once he became better known, opposition would increase. The tenuous Democratic consensus could easily be shattered.[9]

Nor could the Republican candidate be expected to remain so far behind. Until the party met in Kansas City, Gerald Ford was only an accidental President, a contender barely equal to Ronald Reagan in his quest for the nomination, and the heir of Richard Nixon. After his convention victory, Ford had the full majesty of the presidential office, the legitimacy of the party's chosen leader, and the independence conferred by its designation. These new circumstances were quickly reflected in the opinion polls. By the beginning of formal campaigning the President had a limited but real shot at victory.

To maximize his chances, Republican strategists designed a coordinated plan. "The carefully crafted 120-page document advised the President to resist his natural impulse to campaign and instead to stay put in the White House. He lacked the style to win on the hustings; his best bet was to appear presidential while Carter got into trouble on the road." [10] By following this plan, Ford was able to bring the contest back to its basic equilibrium.

THE FORD RUSH

The second phase of the campaign lasted through the month of September and at least through the first week of October. The polls registered a continuous decline in Carter's strength, with the contenders near a standoff by the end of the period. The decline was accelerated by a series of Democratic campaign blunders, which seemed more significant at the time than in a retrospect clouded by the governor's eventual victory. The Democrat's crowds were relatively small, and advance preparations were mismanaged. Different oratorical themes were attempted and then reversed. Ambiguities in policy statements were overanalyzed and often exaggerated by the press.

During this period, the Republicans seized the initiative and turned the campaign from its normal focus, the record of the incumbent administration and party, to an unusual emphasis on the challenger. This vital shift was demonstrated precisely in the first of three televised debates between the presidential candidates. In the first question asked in this debate, Carter mentioned at least eight relatively specific ways to reduce unemployment, including tax revision and the channeling of research funds to central cities. In his rebuttal, the President attacked: "I don't believe that Mr. Carter has been any more specific in this case than he has been on many other issues." [11] By emphasizing the alleged ambiguities in Carter's positions, as well as criticizing his performance as governor of Georgia, Ford was able to refocus the debate—and the campaign—away from his own record.

This shift in emphasis was aided by situational factors, such as tactical errors in the Carter campaign. To be sure, every campaign includes mistakes, but these are commonly forgotten if the candidate wins. Having gained the White House, the Carter campaign may come to be remembered, falsely, as a brilliant effort. In truth, a number of blunders occurred.

The most notorious error was an interview with the governor

that appeared in *Playboy,* a magazine devoted largely to ribald humor and sexually provocative photography. The interview was predominantly a serious portrayal of the candidate and his political views. In a final section, however, Carter sought to allay fears that he would seek to impose his personal moral and religious views on others. He spoke for the "absolute and total separation of church and state" and warned against "pride, that one person should never think he was any better than anybody else." To illustrate his point, he admitted the obvious: "I've looked on a lot of women with lust. I've committed adultery in my heart many times." Recognizing his own mental lapses from absolute morality, the moral lesson was to avoid condemnation of others: "Don't consider yourself better than someone else because one guy screws a whole bunch of women while the other guy is loyal to his wife." [12]

In context, these statements should be read as an honest expression of a tolerant attitude. The effect, however, was to raise doubts about the candidate. The magazine cover—widely publicized by Republicans—promoted such uneasiness. It featured an attractive woman in the act of baring her breasts and the unrelated words "Now, the *real* Jimmy Carter. . . ." Given America's Puritan heritage, the conjunction was hardly likely to emphasize Carter's presidential qualities. Moreover, while adulterous thoughts are virtually universal among adults, the voters expect Presidents to hold to a higher standard, at least publicly.

Ultimately, the interview had little effect on the vote. In the final televised debate, Carter apologized: "If I should ever decide in the future to discuss my deep Christian beliefs and condemnation and sinfulness I'll use another forum besides *Playboy.*" [13] The final polls indicated that few votes were cast in reaction to these words. Yet, in association with other unclear statements, the interview contributed to the general impression of doubt about Carter held by much of the electorate.

The debates, in themselves, further contributed to Ford's upsurge. A debate inherently benefits a trailing candidate, for it puts the contestants on a equal level. All aspects of the debate underline this equality: the same physical arrangements, the same questions asked of each person, the same time alloted to them. These matching arrangements thus tend to reduce any political gap existing between the two debaters.

In the case of Ford and Carter, moreover, the debates not only helped Ford to reduce his deficit, but they also subtly underlined his advantages. The Republican received more deference, being addressed as "Mr. President," in contrast to Carter's humble title of "Governor." Even the Democratic candidate felt a degree of awe and reverence for the presidential office, which limited the severity of his criticisms of Ford. Particularly in the first debate, Carter seemed nervous and uncertain, and was widely acknowledged as the "loser."

Moreover, debates tend to focus on specific details, such as the content of legislative bills. As a sitting President, Ford necessarily would have more knowledge of these matters than a challenger out of office and without federal experience. Again, the result would be to increase impressions of Ford's greater competence and to gain him votes. The debates did not create this difference, of course, because the fact of Ford's incumbency always existed. The joint appearance of the two candidates merely emphasized an existing reality of the 1976 election.

The use of this incumbency was the keystone of Ford's campaign strategy. Americans retain a reverence for the presidential office, an emotion that can be traced to the earliest childhood learning about politics.[14] In the past three administrations, the nation has seen one President assassinated, one driven from office by war, and one forced to resign because of scandal. The hope of the Republicans was that the nation did not want symbolically to kill still another President, through electoral defeat. Ford's peaceful transition to power was emphasized. He virtually ran in opposition to his Republican predecessor, emphasizing the contrast between Nixon's disgrace and his own "decency." The President's television commercials attempted to identify his personal qualities with revered national symbols and an optimistic melody, "I'm feeling good about America." Figuratively and literally, Ford wrapped himself in the Star-Spangled Banner.

Incumbency provided practical as well as symbolic opportunities. While Carter could only promise future policy moves, Ford took such actions daily. For most of the campaign, the President restricted himself to visible but nonpartisan activities, such as signing or vetoing congressional acts, receiving foreign visitors, and holding news conferences. His acts demonstrated his control and his knowledge of government.

Carter would complain about farm prices; Ford would raise government support payments for wheat and milk. Carter would criticize the spread of nuclear material abroad; Ford would announce new restrictions on the sale of plutonium. Carter would advocate fuller support of Israel; Ford would announce a new arms agreement with the Jewish state. Carter would denounce the inequities of the tax system; Ford would sign the tax bill and claim credit for its reforms. Day by day, the message was underlined: Gerald Ford *is* President, Jimmy Carter only *wants* to be.

For 1976, incumbency provided a final, unique advantage. Because of the new election finance law, both candidates were severely restricted in their campaign spending. Each could spend about $25 million, considerably less than the $30 million expended by McGovern four inflationary years earlier, and immensely less than the $60 million available to Nixon. Theoretically, these limits would affect both candidates to the same degree. In fact, however, they may have been more detrimental to Carter. As a challenger, he needed more money than his opponent to make himself and his positions known.

By the end of the campaign, the budget for mass media had become highly restricted, and virtually no funds were available for campaign organization or for such stimulants to political activity as buttons, bumper stickers, and rallies. The Republicans, on the other hand, were able to husband many of their resources for the final weeks of the campaign and for an extensive media effort. In effect, much of their early electioneering was paid through the presidential office. The costs of official functions, aides, and ceremonies were not charged to political funds, but they were an important part of the campaign. Incumbency had both financial and political benefits.[15]

THE FINAL WEEKS

The third phase of the campaign was one of overall stability. The Carter slide was halted, with any additional gains for Ford compensated by other gains for the Democratic challenger. The beginning of this period can be precisely dated, on October 6, the occasion of the second televised debate. Until then, the Ford effort had the appearance of a football team marching relentlessly toward a winning touchdown. After, the game was transformed into a successful goal-line stand by the Democrats, who held on to win.

Immediately after the second debate, much attention was given to Ford's defense of the administration's record of negotiation with the Soviet Union in regard to Eastern Europe. "Each of these countries," Ford argued, is independent, autonomous, it has its own territorial integrity and the United States does not concede that these countries are under the domination of the Soviet Union." His statement was seen as having an immediate adverse impact on voters of Eastern European backgrounds, and Carter exploited the advantage for the next week.[16]

In the actual vote, however, this issue—like other campaign incidents—appeared to have limited impact. More significant was the general effect of the second debate. Even though Ford as President was presumed to be more expert on foreign affairs, he performed less impressively than the former Georgia governor. The initiative of the campaign now switched, as the Republicans were forced onto the defensive. For about ten days, the Ford effort was stalled, with the President attempting to explain away his comment on Eastern Europe. Even though he eventually limited the damage, he had lost an important advantage. Carter now appeared relatively competent in foreign affairs, the flow of voters away from the Democrat had halted, and the governor could return to his previous themes.[17]

For the rest of October, the standoff continued. The polls showed a tight race but were inconsistent on the trend of opinion.[18] As undecided voters made up their minds, Ford appeared to be gaining more adherents, particularly among Independents, Republicans, and those persons concerned with inflation and higher taxes, groups that were always more likely to support the President.

Other factors were promoting Carter's cause. Voters concerned with unemployment as the major national problem, as well as those who perceived a worsening of the economic situation, became more strongly supportive of the Democratic candidate.[19] As statistical indicators showed a pause in the business recovery, the economic issues that had traditionally worked to the advantage of the Democrats became more salient. In a televised debate between the vice-presidential candidates, Democrat Walter Mondale was clearly preferred by the electorate over Republican Robert Dole, providing a supplemental boost to the ticket.[20] A third and final debate between the presidential candidates also resulted in a slight edge for Carter. With these direct confrontations finished, voters were now ready to make a decision.

By Election Day, no pollster and few analysts were willing to make firm predictions of the outcome. A Carter victory nevertheless was in the making. Many voters waited to make their decisions, with a fifth of the electorate still undecided by the last week of the campaign. Once forced to a choice, they tended toward Carter, and "the later a voter made his choice, the more likely he or she was to vote for Carter." He won 53 percent of those deciding in the campaign's final week, and 61 percent of those deciding on the day of the balloting.[21]

The vital last-minute edge for the Democrats was aided by a strong get-out-the-vote effort of labor unions and black organizations and stimulated by the apparent closeness of the vote.[22] As a result, the turnout was greater than expected. Earlier predictions were that fewer than half of those old enough to vote would actually cast their ballots. In fact, almost 54 percent of the population over eighteen went to the polls. The figure was still historically low, even less than that recorded in the runaway contest of 1972, but it was sufficient to bring the majority weight of the Democrats to bear. The close Carter victory margins in states such as Mississippi, Ohio, Pennsylvania, and Texas probably could be attributed to these final efforts.

The historically low turnout in 1976 has been attributed to various causes. One factor mentioned is restrictive registration laws. But these restrictions have actually been eased considerably in recent years, through court decisions, civil rights laws, and such new practices as postcard registration. A more likely cause is the expansion of the electorate to include those aged eighteen to twenty-one. Younger persons have always voted in lower proportions than older citizens.[23] By adding some 35 million potential new voters in 1972 and 1976 from this less active group, the total rate of participation was almost certain to decline.

Another reason for the low turnout is peculiar to the 1976 campaign: the low level of campaign finance. By severely limiting funds for campaign paraphernalia and local organization, past stimulants to voting were removed. Thus the commonly reported "apathy" of the 1976 electorate was probably a reflection, in part, of this lack of the outward hurly-burly of past elections. Finally, there is the widespread feeling of powerlessness. An increasing proportion of Americans believe themselves unable to control the government, which they see as dominated by special interests and uncaring leaders. These feelings are the root cause of nonvoting.[24] Greater turnout will follow not from reforms in registration, but from actions that increase the voters' sense of political efficacy.

Such actions deserve major priority on the agenda of the next administration.

Interpreting the Election

Campaigns are noisy events, even when they are underfunded as in 1976. Noise compels attention, and the noise of a campaign often distracts political observers. But the electoral decision is really a quiet decision, made privately in the voters' minds and hearts, recorded secretly in the isolation of the voting booth. Ultimately the voters withdraw from the sensuous impressions of the campaign: the flickering television images they have seen, the flawed interviews and clumsy remarks they have heard, the outstretched hands they have touched. "Every American election summons the individual voter to weigh the past against the future." [25] So it was in 1976. The choice of Carter and Ford reflected the past and present thinking of the electorate. It also carried important implications for the future of national politics.

PATTERNS IN THE VOTE

In the last analysis, the incidents of the campaign had but limited effects. Rather, the electorate made its decision on four fundamental grounds: party loyalty, basic issues, social class, and evaluation of the candidates.

One of the most striking characteristics of the 1976 vote is its partisan character. For the first time in a generation, the electorate was sharply divided along lines of party loyalty, with Carter gaining four of every five Democrats, and Ford doing even better among the GOP, winning almost nine of every ten Republicans. Since there are almost twice as many Democrats as Republicans in the country, the return to partisanship was critical to Carter's victory.

Partisanship alone can no longer win presidential elections, however, because of the growing numbers of Independents, who now constitute the second largest group in the electorate. For a Republican to win the Presidency, he must carry this vote overwhelmingly. A Democrat, given his party's numerical advantage, needs no better than an even split. Carter met this goal, with estimates of his vote among Independents ranging from 44 to 48 percent. Only Lyndon Johnson, among recent Democratic candidates, has done better.

The reappearance of partisanship as a critical factor in the vote should not be seen as an unthinking return to atavistic party loyalties. Voting research over the past decade has shown that the American voter has become increasingly ideological in his or her partisanship, with the Democrats becoming a predominantly liberal party, the Republicans predominantly conservative. Where issue preferences previously were of limited causal impact on the vote or on party identification, they are now closely associated with both.[26] One illustrative estimate is that the proportion of pure partisan, issueless voters has declined drastically, from 42 percent in 1960 to 23 percent in 1972.[27]

Although detailed analyses must await fuller data, there are already considerable indications that the same relationship exists in 1976 between issue orientation and vote. The electorate divided clearly along lines of self-described ideology, three-fourths of the liberals casting ballots for Carter, and seven of ten conservatives choosing Ford. Comparison to past voting leads to similar conclusions. A major source of Carter's party strength was his winning back to the Democratic party many voters who had bolted to Richard Nixon in 1972. In this election, six of every ten previous defectors returned to the fold. At the same time, Carter held the vote of 90 percent of the Democrats who voted for McGovern. These data suggest—but cannot yet demonstrate—that the most conservative Democrats voted for both Nixon and Ford, while Carter held the liberals who voted for McGovern and recaptured the moderates who temporarily left the party in 1972.

We can speculate that the vote in 1976 may eventually be seen as even more ideological in character than that of 1972. Although McGovern waged an issue-oriented campaign, his support in the voting booth did not fully reflect his efforts. On policy grounds alone, one estimate suggests, McGovern could have won the contest against Nixon. But he failed to mobilize his potential support. "That McGovern could not turn that potential support into actual support may be attributed principally to voter assessments of his personal appeal." [28] Carter, a less controversial and less feared candidate, was able to mobilize the ideological and partisan majority of the Democrats.

The vote was also structured along lines of social class. The clearest correlation among the various demographic breakdowns is that of income and the vote. Carter's strength decreased regularly up the income ladder, as he won nearly two-thirds of the least

economically advantaged voters, while Ford took a similar percentage among those with the highest incomes. In general, this
relationship has existed in American politics since the time of the
social reforms of the New Deal.

In recent years, however, the relationship between income and
voting pattern has become blurred by the growth of Democratic
support among professionals and the attempts of Republicans to
win working-class votes.[29] A glance back at table 3.2 will reveal
that there was relatively little difference in the way persons of
different occupational groupings voted in 1972. Carter's candidacy
reasserted these economic alignments by bringing the Democrats
votes among those of the lower-middle class, in blue-collar occupa-
tions, with high school rather than college education, and in the less
wealthy areas of the South. In 1976, compared to the previous
election, the range of support more than doubled between the upper
and lower rungs of the occupational ladder (a difference of sixteen
percentage points in 1976, compared to seven in 1972). The election may indicate a renewed class basis to American politics.

This possible class basis is also underlined by the importance of
economic issues. The Democrats' success can be attributed to the
fact that at least 8 percent of the labor force was out of work and
that, consequently, unemployment was of great concern to the
voters. In fact, one estimate was that Carter won seven of eight
votes from persons who held unemployment to be the major issue.[30] Since the time of Franklin Roosevelt, the Democratic party
has been seen consistently by the voters as better able to manage
the economy.[31] An uncertain economy brought a focus on these
issues, renewed partisan attachments to the Democratic party, and
gave the election to its nominee. As an Ohio factory worker explained his vote, "I think we need a change; we need a change bad.
I don't especially like Carter, but maybe if we get enough good
Democrats in there to back him up he can do some good." [32]

Ultimately, the choice became one between individuals, and the
voters' perceptions of the personal qualities of Ford and Carter were
important in their decisions. In these personal assessments, Ford
again had the advantages conferred by incumbency. His character
and policies were already known and, even if not always endorsed
by voters, predictable. Stability, experience, and familiarity were
the positive qualities associated with the President, themes his
campaign emphasized. Carter tended to be rated higher on such
qualities as intelligence and compassion. Lacking a record in na-

tional politics, however, voters remained relatively unclear about his personal attributes and policy directions.[33]

Both candidates asked the electorate for "trust"; neither received its firm endorsement. Appreciation of Ford's skill in assuming power after the Nixon resignation was balanced by condemnation of his pardon of the former President. Responsiveness to Carter's moral appeals was balanced by skepticism over his sincerity and consistency. While neither candidate aroused the enmity of the electorate, neither aroused its enthusiasm. The electorate voted out of concern, or from a sense of citizen duty, but not from deep commitment to a man. Narrowly, the voters chose the greater risks and greater opportunities offered by Carter to the safety and pre-dictability presented by Ford. But this choice was not based so much on trust as on hope. The trust necessary for a functioning democracy must still be regained by the American government.

FUTURE PROSPECTS

All events affect the future, and a large-scale event such as a presidential election is especially likely to have long-range implications. Jimmy Carter's victory, therefore, may be more than the choice of a particular man at a particular time. It may also affect the course of American party politics for a generation.

For years before the 1976 election, changes in national politics were apparent. These alterations were evident most dramatically outside the polls: in the rise of protest and direct action as political methods; in the growth of new life styles, especially among the young; in the concern of Americans over questions of war, civil rights, ecology, morality; and in the spread of alienation and distrust. The American political system suffered many shocks, and responded with partial success, partial failure, and partial transformation. Novelty was also evident in the political parties.

The changes were evident in the pattern of party loyalties. In its last period of stability, the decade of the 1950s, the party system securely held the affections of the voters. As many as 90 percent of the electorate would admit that they identified with either the Republicans or the Democrats, or at least "leaned" toward one or the other. Most of those who identified with the parties, moreover, said that they were "strongly" attached to them.[34] These loyalties were of critical importance, leading to the accepted conclusion that "partisanship is the most important single influence on political opinions and voting behavior." [35]

Today, these loyalties have sharply diminished. Independents now represent between a third and two-fifths of the total electorate. Among this group, as many as half decline even to indicate a "leaning" toward the Republicans or Democrats.[36] Thus, those not emotionally identified with the parties now vastly outnumber the approximately 20 percent who consider themselves Republicans, and rival the approximately 40 percent who remain affiliated with the Democrats. There has been a slackening even of these remaining loyalties. "Weak" partisans now outnumber "strong" Democrats and Republicans by a 3–2 margin.

The reduction of party loyalty has also resulted in a lessened impact of these loyalties on the vote itself. Massive defections have occurred in such years as 1964, when a fourth of Republicans deserted Barry Goldwater, and 1972, when two of every five Democrats abandoned George McGovern. The decreasing influence can also be shown statistically. While party loyalty could explain three-fourths of the variation in the vote in 1960, no more than half could be attributed to this factor in 1972.[37] It is likely that the 1976 election will show some reversal of this pattern, since Democrats and Republicans did largely vote for their own party's nominees.[38] However, the results of other recent contests do indicate the potential inconstancy of the voters.

Change has been evident as well in the issues of American politics. Previous party loyalties were built essentially on economic questions, which came into prominence with the Great Depression and the New Deal of Franklin Roosevelt. Their impact could still be detected in the continuing Democratic pluralities formed in the 1930s and in the continuing positive association of the Democratic party with the interests of the working class and the low-wage earner. Over time, however, these issues have faded. They have faded in memory, as those who experienced the traumatic unemployment of the period passed away, and their places in the electorate were taken by their children and grandchildren. The impact of these issues on the vote has faded as well, leaving the Democrats weakened and the political system open to change.[39]

In the period before the 1976 election, new questions began to receive public attention. The international involvement of the United States, particularly in the agony of Vietnam, had disturbed partisan allegiances. Racial conflict and basic questions of racial equality threatened to disrupt the past Democratic coalition of the South, the white working class, and blacks. A whole new set of concerns has involved personal morality and life styles, typified by such issues as legalization of marijuana, women's rights, and amnesty for Vietnam war resisters. Questions of basic social cohesion were raised, including attitudes toward protest activity, toward the maintenance of law and order, and evaluations of such public officials as policemen and the military.

These new issues had altered past patterns and sundered the traditional Democratic majority in 1972. Considerable evidence showed that the electorate was responding to these new issues rather than to the economic alignments established in the era of Franklin Roosevelt.[40] It seemed likely that a new political agenda had been established, from which would follow new party coalitions.[41] While past partisanship did not explain the 1972 vote, these "New Politics" sentiments were quite illuminating. Indeed, the "deviations or discrepancies between expected and observed divisions in the presidential vote are a direct function of New Politics sentiments; the less favorably disposed toward the New Politics, the greater the discrepancy favoring a vote for Nixon." [42]

With the decline of partisanship and the rise of new issues, it seemed possible that the 1976 election would represent a "critical election," one of the great political watersheds of American political history. Such elections occur episodically, about once in a generation, and tend to shape political conflict for the next twenty-five to thirty years. For example, the election of 1896 created the Republican party majority of the early twentieth century, and the elections of 1932 and 1936 created the Democratic majority of Franklin Roosevelt's party.[43]

For the past decade, observers had been predicting another such critical election and a consequent realignment of the major parties. They disagreed, however, on the ultimate result of these predicted changes. Shortly after Nixon's first victory in 1968, one analyst saw the creation of a new Republican majority. Another believed that a revived Democratic coalition would soon come to power. The most thorough investigator, Walter Dean Burnham, cast doubt on the possibility of either political party winning dominance and instead foresaw the continuation of "the onward march of party decomposition." [44]

At this early date after the 1976 election, it is premature even to guess at its ultimate importance. There are some reasons, however, to believe that it does constitute a continuation of the changes that have been increasingly evident in American politics and that it may possibly be seen historically as a critical election. One such reason is time. It has been some forty years since the last major turning point in electoral history. More than one full generation of voters has passed from the scene, with the youngest voters of 1936 now close to drawing their social security pensions. Given this generational replacement, and the immense amount of social change that has occurred in four decades, we would certainly expect political change as well.[45]

We have already noted many signs of such change in 1976. The candidates were different from those of the past, and the ascension of Carter surely represents a shifting of power, both within the Democratic party and in the nation. Defeat of an incumbent President represents another departure from recent history. The voting patterns analyzed above also indicate new alignments. The Democratic candidate received less support from some groups that had been mainstays of the party, while winning new support from other groups.

Of the issues in 1976, questions of life style, morality, and New Politics apparently were subordinated to the established economic questions of inflation and unemployment. Yet this subordination may be only temporary. Economic issues rose to the fore again in 1976 because of the unique combination of a high rate of unemployment and a high rate of inflation. If these rates can be reduced, the newer issues may become prominent again. The growing numbers of younger voters are likely to contribute to such an emphasis. There were also signs of this shift in much of Carter's campaign, in his quasi-religious appeal and his early emphasis on moral concerns. Once in possession of the "bully pulpit" of the White House, the new President may bring renewed public consciousness of such issues.

A shift in political alignment can also be detected through statistical analysis. We can determine the degree of statistical similarity between any two elections by simple correlation of the state-by-state results. In two elections that show similar state coalitions, the Democratic (or Republican) vote in any given state will be similar in the two elections. The result will be a high correlation coefficient, approaching 1.0. If the coalitions in the two elections are not alike, the votes in each state will differ, and the correlation coefficient will be closer to zero. If the alignments are quite different, a negative coefficient will result.[46] Illustratively, if we correlate the results in the 1944 and 1940 elections, we achieve a

Table 3.3

Correlation of Democratic Vote in Selected Presidential Elections, 1928–76

	1976	1972	1968 Humphrey	1968 Humphrey and Wallace
1972	.06	—	.84	−.21
1968 Humphrey	−.00	.84	—	−.18
1968 Humphrey and Wallace	.68	−.21	−.18	—
1964	−.03	.73	.86	−.37
1960	.57	.32	.32	.46
1956	.66	−.31	−.42	.65
1952	.72	−.34	−.33	.84
1948 Truman	.04	.30	.39	−.44
1948 Truman and Thurmond	.54	−.56	−.57	.76
1944	.49	−.55	−.54	.79
1940	.48	−.60	−.60	.75
1936	.36	−.60	−.68	.60
1932	.42	−.60	−.69	.58
1928	.43	−.36	−.38	.66

coefficient of .98, indicating that the two parties were drawing their support in these two contests from the same states.

In table 3.3, the same analysis is performed for a selected group of elections dating back from 1976.[47] The most striking result is how different the Carter-Ford contest is from other recent contests. There is no significant relationship between the vote for Carter in 1976 and that for McGovern in 1972, Humphrey in 1968, or Johnson in 1964.

There appears to have been a significant break in the character of the Democratic coalition in the 1960s, but the changed coalition is not the same as that which brought Carter to victory. Rather, the most recent Democratic success appears different from previous groupings. Its bases are somewhat like that of the Democrats in the New Deal and post-New Deal period, but even these correlations are not overwhelmingly large. It is therefore erroneous to see the

1964	1960	1952	1944	1936
.73	.32	−.34	−.55	−.60
.86	.32	−.33	−.54	−.68
−.37	.46	.84	.79	.60
—	.32	−.39	−.68	−.74
.32	—	.56	.30	.15
−.47	.38	.84	.67	.66
−.39	.56	—	.80	.66
.65	.17	−.16	−.41	−.32
−.68	.21	.78	.94	.90
−.68	.30	.80	—	.91
−.67	.27	.78	.98	.93
−.74	.15	.66	.91	—
−.73	.09	.58	.84	.93
−.56	.22	.58	.82	.76

Carter victory as simply the re-creation of the alliance forged in the elections of Franklin Roosevelt. It is both like and unlike that dominant majority.

The greatest difference from the past is the position of the South. While the Roosevelt coalition included the southern states, these were not its bedrock of support. The Carter coalition is more oriented toward the Georgian's home region. We can see this orientation in the correlations between the 1976 Democratic vote and that of 1948 and 1968. In the latter years, when we add the votes of southern dissidents such as Thurmond in 1948 and Wallace in 1968 to that of the regular Democratic candidate, we achieve much higher correlations. By bringing a new South, one black and white, to the Democratic party, Carter may have forged a new majority coalition.

Future elections will test the durability of this coalition. Until then, we should not simply see the 1976 results as a throwback to the elections of the New Deal. If we seek historical analogies, we probably should go back much further, perhaps to the election of 1828, in which Andrew Jackson won the Democrats' first presidential victory by combining the votes of the South and critical areas of the Northeast. Interestingly, the correlation between the 1976 and 1828 elections is .43, as high as that between 1976 and the contests of the 1930s and 1940s.

The possibility of realignment depends ultimately on the actions of the Carter administration. While the new President did not receive all the votes of the electorate, he is in possession of all the power of the national executive, and therefore able to influence events considerably. It is likely that "the attitudinal change that is associated with realignment is a response to actions by government, actions that are seen by the electorate as successfully dealing with societal problems." [48] The opportunity is now available, with the Democrats controlling all branches. If the new President and his party act to meet the problems of American society, if they win the confidence of the electorate and reverse the trend of increased alienation, then the election of 1976 may be historically significant. It may mark the renewed ascendancy of the Democratic party, the decline of the Republicans to a permanent minority or even their replacement by a new party, and the creation of a new basis of political dispute. It may then become one of the landmarks of American political history—but only the future will provide more certain answers.

CONCLUSION

Whatever its long-run importance, the immediate results of the 1976 election are significant. An incumbent President was defeated, as the voters removed from power the last individuals touched by the Watergate scandals. Blacks came fully into the political system, culminating a period of protest and demands for participation. The nation turned from foreign involvement to a renewed concern for its economic and social problems. A transformed South finally and fully overcame the schism of the Civil War. A new leadership came to office, different in its origins, outlook, and likely programs. Once again, American democracy had proven itself equal to the task of the peaceful transfer of power.

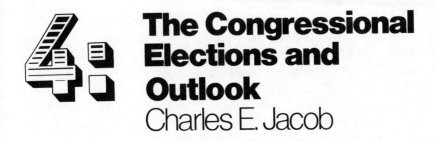

The Congressional Elections and Outlook
Charles E. Jacob

Elections and the New Congress

T first glance it might appear that the 1976 congressional elections were inconsequential. After some 468 separate elections (435 House seats and 33 Senate seats), the net change in party alignment in the two houses is an increase of two Democrats in the House of Representatives and no change in the Senate. The justification for this chapter, of course, rests upon the proposition that there is much more to legislative elections than shifts in the size of majorities and minorities. Nonetheless, we might begin to explore the more complex reality by looking closely at party alignment variations historically.

The 95th Congress, as it assembled in January 1977, divided itself in partisan terms as follows:

House: 292 Democrats, 143 Republicans
Senate: 62 Democrats, 38 Republicans

In national terms it could be said that the electorate restated its preference of the preceding election for overwhelming Democratic party dominance of the legislative process, giving the lower house an extraordinary two-thirds control. (Indeed, the plaint of President Gerald Ford had been that the 94th Congress was a "veto-proof" Congress—a description the inaccuracy of which was pre-

dictable by political analysis and proven by actual experience.)
American political parties as coalitions of ideologically diverse
groupings are an accepted fact of life. Yet these coalitions do have
left-liberal (Democratic) and right-conservative (Republican) centers of gravity, and the numerical weight of one over another tends
to accentuate that center. Moreover, to a President, the force of the
symbolic party tie of his political cohorts is a natural and desirable
target of persuasion. Thus Presidents appreciate Congresses controlled by their partisan brothers. During the past half-century the
usual lack of legislative party control has bedeviled Republican
Presidents. For while the party fortunes have experienced their
ups and downs, only rarely have majorities of Republicans been
returned to office along with Republican Presidents. The last Re-
publican-controlled Congress was the 83rd (1953–55) during President Eisenhower's first half-term. To survey how Congresses have
varied more recently, consider table 4.1.

A number of observations might be made. First, the largest
Democratic majorities in recent years coincided with the Johnson
landslide election of 1964. The first Nixon election of 1968 brought

Table 4.1

Congressional Party Control, 1965–79 [a]

Congress	Years	Partisan alignment		President
95th	1977–79	House:	292 D, 143 R	Carter (D)
		Senate:	62 D, 38 R	
94th	1975–77	House:	291 D, 144 R	Ford (R)
		Senate:	61D, 39 R	
93rd	1973–75	House:	244 D, 191 R	Ford, Nixon (R)
		Senate:	57 D, 43 R	
92nd	1971–73	House:	255 D, 180 R	Nixon (R)
		Senate:	55 D, 45 R	
91st	1969–71	House:	243 D, 192 R	Nixon (R)
		Senate:	58 D, 42 R	
90th	1967–69	House:	248 D, 187 R	Johnson (D)
		Senate:	64 D, 36 R	
89th	1965–67	House:	295 D, 140 R	Johnson (D)
		Senate:	67 D, 33 R	

[a] At election.

sources: *Congressional Quarterly Weekly Report* 34 (6 November 1976):
3123; *Congressional Quarterly Weekly Report* 32 (9 November 1974): 3060;
Congressional Quarterly Weekly Report 30 (11 November 1972): 2952, 2958;
and U.S. Government, *Statistical Abstract of the United States* 93 (1972): 366.

with it only slight increases in the size of the Republican congressional contingent, still a minority in the 91st Congress. The Nixon reelection landslide of 1972 coincided with a Republican House minority increase of only eleven members, and Republican Senate strength actually *decreased* by two. The close Carter victory in 1976 coincided with only the slightest increase in congressional majorities. On the other hand, the midterm elections have shown greater variation. Heavy losses (though not heavy enough to lose a majority) were sustained by Democrats in both houses in the 1966 elections. This accords with the conventional wisdom that the President's party loses at midterm congressional elections. Still, in the 1970 elections, Democrats gained slightly only in the House, where they dropped back in the 1972 presidential year.

THE HOUSE

The 1974 midterm congressional elections are most important to an analysis of the 1976 elections and their meaning. The year 1974 was a Republican washout in Congress. Undoubtedly as a result of Watergate and the presidential resignation, Democrats were elected to Congress, particularly to the House, in huge majorities. Seventy-nine Democratic candidates were elected as freshmen to the 94th Congress.[1] Since this huge influx included many from previously Republican districts and was regarded as a general revolt against Nixonian Republicanism, what happened to these freshmen in 1976 is of particular interest.

What happened as a whole is a testimonial to the potency of incumbency—even the incumbency of a freshman congressman. Consider the overall results in the House.

The 435 House seats of the 94th Congress were up for election. Fifty incumbents retired or, in the case of three, lost primary elections. This left 385 incumbents who contended, of whom 368 were reelected (95.6 percent). Finally, there were 67 new freshmen (47 Democrats and 20 Republicans). For many years, incumbents have been reelected to the House in magnitudes of 90 percent and over, giving rise to the general acceptance of the phenomenon of "incumbent advantage." Yet the loss of only 13 incumbents (8 Democrats, 5 Republicans) of the 94th Congress in 1976 is truly remarkable. Just two years earlier—to demonstrate an exception to the rule of "incumbent advantage"—40 House incumbents were defeated (36 Republicans, 4 Democrats). Nearly all the Republican losers were conservatives associated with President Nixon.

The spectacle of incumbent victories is even more striking among those 79 Democratic freshmen of the "Class of '74": 78 sought reelection, and 76 were victorious. Of the two Democratic incumbents who lost, one, Representative Allan Howe of Utah, had been involved in a preelection scandal involving the alleged solicitation of prostitutes; the other, Representative Tim Hall of Illinois, simply could not withstand the combination of a traditional, conservative Republican district in central Illinois and the overall Republican victory in the state.[2]

One result of the 1976 elections is a very junior House of Representatives. Relected one-term incumbents plus 67 new freshmen constitute over one-third of the House membership. Put another way, somewhat more than a majority of the whole House in the 96th Congress have come to Congress since 1972. The possible impact of the "juniors" will be discussed later in this chapter. Let us now look more closely at the results of the Senate elections in 1976.

THE SENATE

Elections to the Senate in 1976 present a counter-theme to the House experience of the triumph of incumbency. While party alignment in the Senate of the 95th Congress is exactly the same as its predecessor, there are more new members (18) than at any time since 1948. And more incumbents (9) were defeated than in any election since that year. The raw results may be outlined as follows: 33 seats were up for election. Of these, 8 members voluntarily retired, leaving 25 incumbents contesting. Of these, 9 were defeated. Thus the Senate incumbent reelection success rate was only 64 percent, compared with over 95 percent in the House.

The great proportion of those defeated fall into two tenure categories. Seven out of the nine losers were members of either the Democratic "Class of '58" seeking a fourth term, or the Republican "Class of '70" seeking a second term (see table 4.2).

The Democratic "Class of '58" was seventeen strong, swept in on the surging Democratic congressional tide that rose at midterm of the second Eisenhower administration. Of that original group, seven survived to 1976, when three of them were denied a fourth term. It will be recalled that 1970 was the midterm election in which Republicans increased their strength (though still a minority) in the Senate. Of the six new Republican senators of that year, four were denied a second term in 1976. Only William Roth

Table 4.2
*Defeated Senate Incumbents, 1976*_____

Member	Party	State	Terms served
Hartke	Dem.	Ind.	3
McGee	Dem.	Wyo.	3
Moss	Dem.	Utah	3
Montoya	Dem.	N.M.	2
Tunney	Dem.	Cal.	· 1
Beall	Rep.	Md.	1
Brock	Rep.	Tenn.	1
Buckley	Rep.	N.Y.	1
Taft	Rep.	Ohio	1

SOURCE: *Congressional Quarterly Weekly Report* 34 (6 November 1976): 3127–28.

of Delaware and Lowell Weicker of Connecticut survived to a second term. It is noteworthy that Weicker, largely due to his conduct on the Watergate Committee, was perceived as anti-Nixon, and Roth was never closely associated with the administration. On the other hand, the four defeated Republicans were in varying degrees supporters of the President and politically supported by him. It appears that the retaliation of the electorate against the Nixon loyalists, which began in the House elections of 1974, continued to conclusion in 1976.

Of course there were other reasons for these defeats—individual, idiosyncratic factors. For example, James Buckley of New York, originally elected by a plurality as the Conservative candidate in a three-way race, hardly seemed representative of the political tendencies of his statewide constituency. In the cases of Glenn Beall, Bill Brock, and Robert Taft, each won his first term narrowly and had a track record that showed vulnerability.[3]

Among the Democratic losers, both Joseph Montoya and John Tunney had other kinds of problems. Montoya had to contend with a cloud of suspicion raised about his personal business and tax affairs; Tunney was apparently unable to overcome his image as a "lightweight" and "playboy." [4] And both faced colorful opponents: Montoya, a former astronaut (Harrison Schmitt) and Tunney, a septuagenarian who was a culture hero in some quarters (S. I. Hayakawa).

A more general consideration of the impact of the stages of a senatorial career may offer a partial explanation for the results of

1976. Donald Matthews, in a study of the Senate published some years ago, perceived a senatorial life cycle in connection with a senator's relations with his constituency.[5] Matthews studied the careers of senators serving in the 1947–57 period and found certain electoral patterns. Once elected, a senator, unlike his counterpart in the House, has a six-year lease on office. During this time he may build on initial constituency support, applying all the advantages of incumbency. Given the substantial resources attending the office —publicity, allowances, and the ability to perform services for his state—along with relatively small leadership and initiative-taking responsibilities *within* the Senate, the freshman can concentrate on "nursing" his constituency. If he is successful in these areas, he may even be able to overcome the disadvantage of a competitive party system in the state or negative circumstances in the larger political and economic environment over which he may have limited control. Still, surviving the first term is the crucial challenge. Once reelected, Matthews found that the opportunity for going on successfully to a third term is greatly enhanced.

Then the next stage of the cycle comes into focus. By the beginning of the third term, typically, the senator is compelled to assume more internal, institutional responsibilities, which seniority mandates in the Senate. He is a high-ranking member of several committees, possibly even a chairman. Surely he will chair one or more subcommittees. He may have some party leadership responsibilities. His relationships with the President and executive branch become increasingly involved. He often pays less attention to his constituency. Fences sometimes go unmended. Local opposition groups are encouraged. The result, Matthews found, was that upon approaching the fourth-term contest a senator is less secure than at any time after his first term: "Beyond a third term, the senior senator has less chance of gaining re-election than a freshman!" [6]

In 1976 it may well be that the three members of the Democratic "Class of '58" who were defeated found their statistical place in succumbing to the disadvantages of seniority. Indeed, among the four winners of fourth terms, the case of Edmund Muskie is instructive. In early 1976 the senior senator from Maine was in trouble, and the major source of this trouble was that Muskie had become increasingly estranged from his constituency. He was commonly seen by Maine voters as too preoccupied with national leadership to give his home state due attention. It took a season of intensive fence-mending and the help of a weak opponent to bring the senator comfortably to a fourth-term victory.

The other three Democratic winners of fourth terms present classic cases of invulnerable presences. Robert Byrd of West Virginia, a Senate party leader and candidate for the majority leadership in the 95th Congress, was even spared the nuisance of an opponent. Harrison Williams of New Jersey abetted his substantial support from organized labor in his state by a personal upsurge in his attention to state matters prior to the campaign; in addition he was challenged by a young, unknown, underfinanced opponent. Williams won 62 percent of the vote, even though President Ford carried the state. Finally, Howard Cannon of Nevada rode to an easy fourth-term victory (64 percent) in spite of a conflict-of-interest charge, which was his opponent's only sustained issue.[7]

COATTAILS AND TICKET-SPLITTING

A factor that is always of interest in congressional elections that coincide with presidential elections is the relationship between the two. A persistent thesis of political science suggests that a coattail effect should appear. The theory rests on the strength of party identification, however, and this has clearly declined in recent years. It was once supposed that the presidential candidate—being the main attraction and appearing at the top of the ballot in any constituency—would help candidates of his party farther down the list. That is, the *partisan* choice at the outset would be crucially important to subsequent voter choices for other offices. This could be particularly true in jurisdictions that provided for voting the "straight ticket" in one act.[8]

But there is an antithesis to the coattail thesis: the phenomenon of ticket-splitting, or voting for candidates of different parties in different offices. Only an examination of the actual voting choices in any election will disclose the impact of either coattails or ticket-splitting. For present purposes, let us sample the relationship between presidential and congressional choices by looking more closely at the thirty-three senatorial elections that occurred across the country (see table 4.3).

In these races, Democratic senatorial candidates won 21, Republicans won 11, and Independent Harry Byrd of Virginia won one. At the presidential level, Ford won 17 of the states, and Carter won 16. As we look at the individual contests we find that in 10 of

Table 4.3
*Senate and Presidential Majorities in 1976*_____

State	Winning senate party (in percent)	Winning presidential party (in percent)
Arizona	55 D	57 R
California	50 R	50 R
Connecticut	58 R	52 R
Delaware	56 R	52 D
Florida	62 D	53 D
Hawaii	57 D	51 D
Indiana	59 R	54 R
Maine	60 D	49 R
Maryland	57 D	53 D
Massachusetts	70 D	56 D
Michigan	53 D	53 R
Minnesota	68 D	56 D
Mississippi	[a] D	50 D
Missouri	57 R	51 D
Montana	64 D	54 R
Nebraska	53 D	59 R
Nevada	64 D	53 R

[a] No opponent in race.

SOURCE: *Congressional Quarterly Weekly Report* 34 (6 November 1976): 3118, 3147–54.

the 17 states won by Ford, the *Democratic* senatorial candidate was victorious. And 4 of the 16 states won by Carter elected *Republican* senators. Including the Independent candidate, there were thus 15 instances of ticket-splitting between presidential and senatorial choices—or nearly half the elections.

Further, if we look to those states where presidential and senatorial candidates of the same party did win, we can examine the relative margins of victory for evidence of any coattail effect. Of the seven states won by President Ford *and* Republican senate candidates, the President's margin was greater than that of the senator in four states. Perhaps in three of these (Utah, Wyoming, and Vermont) the President helped, particularly in Vermont where Senator Robert Stafford won by only about 50 percent and the President won by 55 percent in a small electorate. The California case is very doubtful as a demonstration of coattails, for Ford gar-

State	Winning senate party (in percent)	Winning presidential party (in percent)
New Jersey	62 D	50 R
New Mexico	57 R	51 R
New York	55 D	52 D
North Dakota	62 D	52 R
Ohio	51 D	50 D
Pennsylvania	53 R	51 D
Rhode Island	58 R	56 D
Tennessee	53 D	56 D
Texas	57 D	52 D
Utah	54 R	64 R
Vermont	50 R	55 R
Virginia	57 IND	51 R
Washington	74 D	51 R
West Virginia	a D	58 D
Wisconsin	73 D	50 D
Wyoming	55 R	60 R

nered only a handful of votes more than Hayakawa. In the three remaining Republican states (Connecticut, Indiana, and New Mexico), Ford ran behind the senatorial candidates.

In the case of candidate Carter, evidence of coattails is almost nonexistent. Of the twelve states that went Democratic in both contests, Carter ran ahead of the senate candidate in only one. As *Congressional Quarterly* has noted, Carter may have helped Democratic candidate James Sasser in Tennessee: Carter won by 200,000 votes, and Sasser won by only about 80,000.[9] In the other eleven states, Carter ran behind the senators, in some states far behind. For example, in Wisconsin, Carter won by only 40,000 votes while Senator William Proxmire garnered an 850,000-vote victory (73 percent). In Ohio, another state whose crucial electoral votes were won by Carter with only 7,500 votes to spare out of nearly 4,000,000, Howard Metzenbaum won by 118,000.

The clear verdict of 1976 was that widespread voter discrimination by ticket-splitting left little room for presidential coattails as a variable helping to explain the results of congressional elections.

The New Congress: Behavioral Expectations

In examining the new Congress, one is interested in such things as its potential effectiveness as a legislative body, the political ideological tendencies that are likely to predominate, and the nature of its relationships with the President in the enactment of public policies. This section looks at some relevant evidence in the search for clues that might help to predict future directions.

EXPERIENCE

Particularly in recent decades, the Congress has been characterized as a body of political professionals. That is, the great proportion of its members have been people who moved into national legislative office after a considerable apprenticeship in politics and public office at state and local levels. Moreover, upon arriving in Congress—especially in the House of Representatives—members tended to stay on, making a career on Capitol Hill. Indeed, just a few years ago, the *average* tenure of members of the House was eleven years. Long tenure, along with other internal factors, gave rise to discussions about the institutionalization of the House of Representatives.[10] The fact that a majority of the new House has come to office since 1972, however, suggests that the reign of stability and institutional conservatism is likely to continue to be challenged, as it has been during the past two Congresses. This countertrend is also evident in the Senate, where retirements in 1976 were at the highest level since before World War II,[11] and the defeat of incumbents in November resulted in nearly one-fifth of that body being newcomers.

But what of the political experience of the new members of Congress? Background information on these freshmen indicates that the path to Washington remains marked by stopovers at the statehouse, mayor's office, or city council chamber, though this is more true of senators, as might be expected, than freshmen congressmen (see table 4.4).

We see that two-thirds of House freshmen and more than four-fifths of freshmen senators have been engaged in politics prior to

Table 4.4
Prior Political Experience of Freshmen in Congress————————

Senate

	Freshmen	National level	State and local	None
	10 D	6	4	0
	8 R	1	4	3
Total	18	7	8	3

House

	Freshmen	Prior experience	Percent	None	Percent
	47 D	35	74	12	26
	20 R	9	45	11	55
Total	67	44	66	23	34

SOURCE: *Congressional Quarterly Weekly Report* 34 (9 October 1976): 2771–2869.

election to their present offices. The partisan breakdown is interesting; it shows that Democratic freshmen are more professional than their Republican counterparts. The Senate had no inexperienced Democrats, and six of them had served in national positions before election to the Senate. Undoubtedly the best-known of these is Daniel Patrick Moynihan of New York, who served in a number of executive, cabinet, and ambassadorial positions under Presidents since John Kennedy. Four new Democrats succeeded in promoting themselves from the House (Spark Matsunaga, Paul Sarbanes, Donald Riegle, John Melcher), and Howard Metzenbaum served in the Senate in the early 1970s.

Among Republican freshmen senators, only H. J. Heinz of Pennsylvania has prior national experience, having served three terms in the House. What is striking, of course, is that three freshmen Republicans are total newcomers to the political scene. Hayakawa of California had been an educator and university administrator; Schmitt of New Mexico was an astronaut; and Orrin Hatch of Utah is a Salt Lake City attorney who simply decided to run for the Senate as a self-styled "free enterprise conservative." [12]

Let us suppose that effectiveness in Congress is related to an acquaintance with the political skills of bargaining and negotiation and a familiarity with complex institutional structure that provides a sense of place. Then one would anticipate that the freshmen Democrats—particularly those who have held national office—will be at an advantage that exceeds the mere strength of numbers of their partisan cohorts in Congress.

LIBERALISM AND CONSERVATISM IN THE NEW SENATE

Positions on the great issues of American politics are conventionally polarized between traditional tendencies toward liberalism or conservatism. To be sure, these ideological labels are not exact. Much philosophical debate about what really *is* the liberal or conservative position on particular issues is a commonplace of political dialogue. Yet the distinctions are useful; more important, most political figures think of themselves as predominately one or the other, and this self-designation has much to do with their actual behavior.

In Congress, granting the exceptions that always exist, liberals *tend* to be more open to social and political experimentation than their conservative counterparts. They *tend* to favor domestic social welfare and economically redistributive programs as against the normal conservative suspicion of such thrusts. They *tend* to tolerate a larger role for the federal government and freer government spending. Conservatives have an ingrained skepticism about big government and advocate a tighter rein on the public treasury.

Unable to examine in necessary depth the liberal or conservative behavior of every congressman and senator, the political analyst seeks shortcuts, indicators of ideological placement. The most common of these shortcuts is an examination of the evaluations of legislative behavior made by groups that define themselves as standard-bearers of ideological positions. Several such groups routinely monitor the voting records of every legislator each year. Among them are the chief liberal groups—Americans for Democratic Action (ADA) and Committee on Political Education of the American Federation of Labor–Congress of Industrial Organizations (COPE)—and the chief conservative groups—Americans for Constitutional Action (ACA) and Chamber of Commerce of the United States (CCUS). Each year these groups select about twenty major issues before Congress, define the "correct" ideological position on the issue, and score the legislators on whether or not they conform to the liberal or conservative position.

The 1975 scores awarded for liberalism by the ADA will be

examined for those members of the Senate who resigned, retired, or were defeated in 1976. Ten Democrats and eight Republicans fell into this category. And they were replaced by ten freshmen Democrats and eight freshmen Republicans. The purpose is to find the extent of ideological change independent of partisanship and therefore make an inference about the ideological quality of the new freshmen class in the Senate.

There is a difficulty in comparison, however. Nearly all the freshmen senators do *not* have ADA scores because most of them did not hold positions rated by ADA before entering the Senate. We shall try to surmount this difficulty by reference to another indicator of ideology. This is the evidence of support given by several ideological groups to the campaigns of the senatorial candidates. This support took the form of endorsement, financial contributions, and general electioneering. There are eight such groups, four liberal and four conservative. ADA and COPE are represented among the four liberal support groups, and ACA is represented among conservative support groups. In addition, on the liberal side, the United Auto Workers and the National Committee for an Effective Congress were active. On the conservative side, the three additional groups were the Business-Industry Political Action Committee, Committee for the Survival of a Free Congress, and National Conservative Political Action Committee.[13] Table 4.5 lists the nature of support, liberal or conservative, and the number of groups supporting each freshman elected.

It can be seen at a glance that all Democratic winners had some liberal group support, although Edward Zorinsky of Nebraska could arouse the enthusiasm of only one such group. This is not surprising; Zorinsky is a former Republican and conducted a very conservative campaign in his state. Among the Republicans, only Senator Heinz could attract *no* conservative group support in his race in Pennsylvania. Again, not surprising. Heinz has been a moderate-to-liberal congressman for three terms and received a score of 68 percent from ADA in his most recent rating.[14]

Some interesting transformations in Senate representation from particular states are evident. The very liberal Senator Tunney of California was replaced by a self-declared conservative, Hayakawa, who had maximum support from conservative groups. The reverse happened in New York where Mr. Conservative (Buckley) was defeated by the cosmopolitan Daniel Moynihan, who conducted a campaign based upon liberal themes and had strong liberal group

Table 4.5
*Ideology and Succession in the Senate*_____

State	Defeated incumbent	ADA rating	Winner	Support groups
Indiana	Hartke (D)	72	Lugar (R)	C, 3
Wyoming	McGee (D)	39	Wallop (R)	C, 3
Utah	Moss (D)	61	Hatch (R)	C, 4
New Mexico	Montoya (D)	44	Schmitt (R)	C, 3
California	Tunney (D)	83	Hayakawa (R)	C, 4
Maryland	Beall (R)	44	Sarbanes (D)	L, 4
Tennessee	Brock (R)	22	Sasser (D)	L, 4
New York	Buckley (R)	0	Moynihan (D)	L, 3
Ohio	Taft (R)	22	Metzenbaum (D)	L, 4

	Retired		*Successor*	
Michigan	Hart (D)	61	Riegle (D)	L, 4
Missouri	Symington (D)	72	Danforth (R)	C, 1
Montana	Mansfield (D)	83	Melcher (D)	L, 4
Rhode Island	Pastore (D)	67	Chafee (R)	C, 1
Minnesota	Mondale (D)	94	Anderson (D) [a]	—
Arizona	Fannin (R)	11	DeConcini (D)	L, 4
Hawaii	Fong (R)	22	Matsunaga (D)	L, 4
Nebraska	Hruska (R)	6	Zorinsky (D)	L, 1
Pennsylvania	Scott (R)	39	Heinz (D)	None

[a] Senator Wendell Anderson, Minnesota, succeeded on Senator Mondale's resignation to assume the vice-presidency.

SOURCE: *Congressional Quarterly Weekly Report* 34 (22 May 1976): 1291–93; and idem (6 November 1976): 3139.

support. Similarly, in Maryland, Senator Sarbanes, who had a 100 percent ADA rating in 1975 in the House, replaced conservative Beall.

In sum, the ideological complexion of the new Senate has not changed drastically from its predecessor. On balance, however, it might be argued that the new Senate will turn out to be a somewhat more liberal body. One way of interpreting the net effect of the changes in personnel is as follows: Seven of the departed senators had high ADA scores (over 60 percent). Ten of the freshmen senators had combinations of strong liberal support groups and high ADA ratings in the House. On the other hand, ten of the departed senators had low ADA scores, but only seven freshmen had the endorsement or support of conservative groups in the campaign. Thus, while the partisan division in the new Senate is the same as before, the extrapartisan factor of ideology may operate in favor of the already extraordinary Democratic majority.

LIBERALISM AND CONSERVATISM IN THE NEW HOUSE

Of the 63 incumbents of the House who either retired (50) or were defeated (13), 28 were strong supporters of the liberal ADA position, using the 60 percent cutting point. As would be expected, 24 of these were Democrats, and only 4 were Republicans. In any case, less than half of those who departed could be considered liberal by the usual standards.[15]

The 95th Congress has 67 freshmen (47 Democrats, 20 Republicans) about whose ideological tendencies we can only speculate. Yet if we can once again apply the maxim that a person is known by the friends he keeps, campaign group support levels for these freshmen may serve as an indicator. The same four liberal and four conservative groups surveyed in the case of Senate freshmen endorsed and supported House candidates. Table 4.6 reflects the sentiments of these groups in 1976.

In the case of House freshmen, 87 percent of Democrats elected had liberal group support, the average candidate having had the support of two such groups. Among freshmen Republicans, 90

Table 4.6
Group Support for House Freshmen

All candidates	N	%	Democrats groups	N	%	Republicans groups	N	%
Group support								
Four groups	6	9	L, 4	3	6	C, 4	3	15
Three groups	17	25	L, 3	14	30	C, 3	3	15
Two groups	23	34	L, 2	16	34	C, 2	7	35
One group	13	20	L, 1	8	17	C, 1	5	25
No groups	8	12		6	13		2	10
Total:	67	100		47	100		20	100

SOURCE: *Congressional Quarterly Weekly Report* 34 (6 November 1976): 3139–44.

percent had conservative group support, again the average member garnering the support of two such groups. It is, of course, impossible to infer that the expectations of group supporters will be proportionately rewarded by approved ideological behavior on the part of new legislators. Yet, in only 12 percent of the candidacies were ideological interest groups unwilling to place their bets. One conclusion that seems plausible in terms of net effect rests upon the shattering, better than 2–1 superiority of Democratic numbers. If the law of chance ordains that the liberally supported Democrat will behave liberally in Congress about as often as the conservatively supported Republican acts like a conservative in Congress, then these freshmen will, on balance, tilt in the liberal direction.

Scanning more selectively across the 95th Congress, the 76 Democratic freshmen incumbents who were reelected in 1976 deserve special attention. Elected in the anti-Nixon surge of 1974, many from traditionally Republican districts, nearly everyone survived to reelection in 1976. Thus their large numbers and their ideological tendencies give them great significance in the 95th Congress. And their past behavior illustrates a disproportionately liberal inclination.

In 1975 in the House of Representatives, 113 members (110 Democrats, 3 Republicans) received scores of 80 percent or better on the ADA charts. This compares to only 65 members who classified as strong liberals in 1974. Of these 110 Democrats, 43 of the high scorers were freshmen. Indeed, 12 freshmen Democrats received scores of 100 percent on the ADA liberalism ratings. It should also be noted that 12 of the 18 Republican freshmen of the 94th Congress scored 80 percent or better on the conservative ACA charts. But again, partisan numbers make the difference— 43 (Democratic) liberals as against 12 (Republican) conservatives. Using another liberal index, in 1975 some 192 congressmen scored 80 percent or better on the COPE list of liberal bellwether votes. Of these, 55 were *freshmen* Democrats.[16]

A phenomenon of the Congress for at least the past forty years, and one that throws into bold relief the distinction between partisan polarities and ideological polarities, is the presence of the "conservative coalition." Since the early days of the Roosevelt New Deal, conservative northern Republicans and conservative southern Democrats have made common cause in opposing the policy direction of the generally liberal, northern Democratic leadership

Table 4.7
*The Conservative Coalition in the House of Representatives,
1969–76*

Year	Percent appearances on recorded votes	Percent victories
1969	27	71
1970	22	70
1971	30	79
1972	27	79
1973	23	67
1974	24	67
1975	28	52
1976	22	59

SOURCE: *Congressional Quarterly Weekly Report* 34 (24 January 1976): 170; and idem (30 October 1976): 3100.

and its supporters. In truth this has often resulted in a virtual three-party system in Congress.

The conservative coalition comes together only on votes that clearly pose conservative principles at odds with liberal principles (most *major* issues). According to the operational definition of the Congressional Quarterly Service, the conservative coalition acts when a voting alliance appears between Republicans and southern Democrats opposing northern Democrats. A conservative coalition vote on a particular issue is one associated with the above alliance. The sum of any congressman's votes in accord with the conservative coalition alignment produces a conservative coalition support score.[17] Reverse behavior produces a conservative coalition opposition score. To provide some picture of the role of the conservative coalition in the Nixon and Ford administrations, consider table 4.7.

Returning to our concern with the behavior of the Democratic freshmen class in the 94th Congress, we find that they were more liberal than their Democratic colleagues in terms of their support for and opposition to the conservative coalition. Whereas all House Democrats supported the coalition 34 percent of the time in 1975, freshmen Democrats supported it only 27 percent of the time. Moreover, the *opposition* scores of freshmen House Democrats were also the highest, running to 69 percent.[18] Assuming no radical change in ideological preference and voting behavior, one can anticipate a very substantial bloc of pro-liberal, anti-conservative votes from the 76 freshmen Democrats who were returned to office in the 1976 congressional elections.

The New Congress and the New President

Directions in the new Congress—whether it is effective or ineffective, whether its work is touched by liberal or conservative impulses, whether it strengthens or weakens support for the entire political system—will be shaped in large measure by the body's symbiotic relationship with the President. For in contemporary American politics, the legislative process is one shared by 535 legislators and the President. Modern Congresses demand legislative leadership from Presidents, and Presidents must work for support from Congresses. A productive relationship depends upon the skill of the President in applying the arts of persuasion [19] and the ability and will of the legislators to respond. The interplay of partisan support, legislative institutional arrangements, and issue priorities is crucial to a rewarding consummation of public policy.

THE LEGISLATIVE PARTIES

A major measurement of the stature of any Presidency is the extent to which the Chief Executive succeeds in convincing Congress to enact his policies. In the attempt, Presidents must rely primarily upon legislative support from among their partisans and secondarily on support from the opposition party. Logic would suggest that the greater the size of the majority of the President's party in Congress, the better are his chances of success. Reciprocally, it would seem that when the President's party is in the minority in Congress, his programs will suffer. Logic is *generally* borne out by experience. Table 4.8 portrays the relative success of five Presidents over the past fourteen Congresses. Success is determined by the extent to which Presidents achieved legislative passage of their policy recommendations.[20]

Perhaps the most striking conclusion from these data is that, even when the President is beleaguered by the minority status of his party in Congress, he will always succeed more than half the time and might generally expect to succeed in seeing two out of every three of his positions accepted. However, when the President's party *controls* Congress—even narrowly, as in the first

Table 4.8

Presidential Success and Congressional Majorities _____

Administration	Years	Success (percent)	Congress	Party House Majority (percent)	Party Senate Majority (percent)
Eisenhower (R)	1953–54 *	85.9	83rd	R, 50.8	R, 50
	1955–56	72.5	84th	D, 53.3	D, 50
	1957–58	69	85th	D, 53.5	D, 51
	1959–60	58.5	86th	D, 66	D, 65
Kennedy (D)	1961–62 *	83.2	87th	D, 60.4	D, 65
	1963 *	87.1	88th	D, 59.3	D, 68
Johnson (D)	1964 *	88	88th	D, 59.3	D, 67
	1965–66 *	86	89th	D, 67.8	D, 68
	1967–68 *	77	90th	D, 56.7	D, 64
Nixon (R)	1969–70	75.5	91st	D, 55.8	D, 57
	1971–72	70.5	92nd	D, 58.6	D, 54
	1973–74	55	93rd	D, 56	D, 57
Ford (R)	1974	58.2	93rd	D, 56	D, 57
	1975–76	57.4	94th	D, 67	D, 61
Carter (D)	1977–78 *	?	95th	D, 67	D, 62

* Designates years in which Congress and President are of the same party.

SOURCE: *Congressional Quarterly Weekly Report* 34 (30 October 1976): 3092; idem 30 (11 November 1972): 2952, 2958; idem 32 (9 November 1974): 3064, 3068; and *Statistical Abstract of the United States, 1972,* p. 366.

Eisenhower term—his programs pass, on average, 85 percent of the time.

The data further suggest that the *size* of congressional majorities has some bearing on presidential success. Thus, when the size of the Democratic majority shrank significantly in 1967, Lyndon Johnson's success rate declined. On the other hand, when the President's party is already in the minority, modest shifts in size do not seem to affect presidential success greatly, as in the Nixon years. Moreover, cataclysmic events seem to have an impact on presidential success that transcends congressional majorities. Lyndon Johnson's low point (1967–68) coincided with the Vietnam agony; Nixon's low point (1973–74) reflected Watergate.

From an exclusively congressional perspective, the outlook for the Carter administration in the 95th Congress is promising. Not since the halcyon days of Lyndon Johnson's Great Society Congress (1965–66) has a President had a majority the size of Jimmy Carter's. Whether Mr. Carter can exploit these majorities to maximum benefit depends in part on the way the majorities are organized within Congress. This is a matter that merits exploration.

STRUCTURES OF POWER

In his relations with Congress, the President must influence and treat with two foci of internal power: the party legislative leadership and a collectivity of chairmen of the standing committees.[21] In the case of Democratic party leadership, President Carter should be able to depend upon the loyalty and general popularity of Speaker Tip O'Neill of the House and upon the liberally oriented majority leadership. In the Senate, Majority Leader Robert Byrd, while not a dynamic liberal, has made a career (most recently as chief whip) of being a party-line stalwart. Even in the contests for either of the majority leadership posts, no serious candidate fell beyond the fringe of Democratic liberal centrism.

The committee chairmen present a greater and more complex challenge. As a result of the great legislative turnover of the past two years, many committee chairmanships have been reshuffled, particularly in the House. This is not likely to make a great difference, for two reasons. First, the most influential chairmanships in both houses remain stable. Second, changes in the chairmanships give no evidence of significant change in the orientations of the committees.[22]

Congressmen George Mahon of Texas and Al Ullman of Oregon continue to preside over the money committees—Appropriations and Ways and Means respectively. In each case, these men and their committees have the potential and probable inclination to contest with the President should his programs, particularly taxing and domestic spending programs, appear fiscally overambitious. Even before the inauguration, President-elect Carter's early statements about the possibility of a tax cut in 1977 underwent a softening reformulation after Chairman Ullman expressed some strong reservations. In the Senate, the story is repeated. Powerful finance Committee Chairman Russell Long of Louisiana and Appropriations committee Chairman John McClellan of Arkansas continue a conservative domination over priority-setting money bills. (In 1975 McClellan's ADA rating was 6 percent, and Long's was 22 percent.)

Beyond the possible obstacles to presidential dominance that may arise from ideological differences, the spirit of the Congress as an institution that has developed over the past few years could result in rebuffs to executive leadership. After a considerable period during which Congress was regarded, and regarded itself, as a rather weak adjunct to executive policy-making purpose, the legislators increasingly are recapturing a fuller measure of their historic prerogatives. This has come about in two ways.

Congress, having realized that a large measure of its weakness was its own responsibility, engaged in a series of internal institutional reforms and self-evaluations. Was it undemocratic? It proceeded to make assaults on the seniority system in the House, and in 1975 the Democratic Caucus actually deposed three committee chairmen. Was it overly secretive? It opened up its committee hearings to public scrutiny and introduced recorded teller voting in the House. Was it inefficient—most egregiously in the handling of its most important business, money matters? It responded in 1974 by establishing Congressional Budget Committees with the power to present a systematic and authoritative congressional budget. Did it fail to exercise proper administrative oversight? It began more zealously to employ its investigating committees and the General Accounting Office. In short, Congress has gone a long way toward getting its houses in order.

The other wellspring of a revivified Congress has resulted from its executive target of opportunity. Perhaps it took the excesses of the Nixon Presidency to prompt a retaliatory spirit in Congress. In any case, the imposition of controls on executive impoundments of appropriated funds is a case of Congress striking back, as is the War Powers Act, intended to harness presidential foreign policy adventurism. So, too, is the increased resort to a "legislative veto," whereby the lawmakers write an act with particular provisions that can be implemented only with additional legislative approval. In each of these ways Congress in the mid-1970s has reasserted itself. And each mode of reassertion has been fueled by large turnovers in membership, bringing to its ranks young, active, reform-minded lawmakers unsocialized to the traditional, conservative norms of the chambers.[23] There is opportunity in this phenomenon for a skilled, discreet, and cooperative President. There is the potential for frustration for a stubborn and overly assertive President.

ISSUES

In the absence of an unexpected foreign policy crisis, the major issues over which President and lawmakers will contend in the 95th Congress will be domestic concerns. One might predict even more narrowly that these will be largely the economic issues stressed in the 1976 election. The problems sometimes referred to as "social issues" were largely ignored in the presidential contest and seem to have disappeared from the public agenda.

Unemployment, inflation, and taxes were the areas of concern highlighted in candidate Carter's presidential campaign. On the cutting question of choice between continued high unemployment or lowered inflation, Carter seemed to align himself with the liberal legions and would make the hard choice of reducing unemployment even at the expense of greater inflation. Yet Carter was not unambiguous on the question. He supported the substance of the Humphrey-Hawkins bill before Congress in 1976. That "full employment" bill would have mandated a 3 percent reduction of unemployment within four years or committed the federal government to provide public jobs. However, Humphrey-Hawkins failed in the 94th Congress and remains controversial in the 95th. Mr. Carter is aware of this and probably will support some more limited jobs program.[24]

On the tax question, Carter has repeatedly referred to the present tax system as a "national disgrace" and has called for a truly comprehensive reworking of the federal tax structure to achieve a more progressive direction. However, in 1976 Congress passed a major tax revision measure and is unlikely to depart from its usual leisurely interval in 1977–78 to take up the tax question again. Moreover, Mr. Carter had said that tax reform is not an immediate project for 1977.[25]

During the 1976 campaign, Carter drew the fervent support of consumer groups, including the aloof Ralph Nader. His major proposal was for a Consumer Advocacy Agency, its organizational predecessor having been vetoed by President Ford. In addition, Carter expressed himself in favor of a national no-fault insurance law and the legitimation of class-action suits.[26] Such matters may find themselves once again on the legislative agenda in 1977.

One of the issues Mr. Carter has discussed most extensively is a domestic governmental issue: executive branch reorganization. As the former "outsider," he deplored the waste, inefficiency, and duplication found in the federal bureaucracy and promised to reorganize top-to-bottom to provide for a more efficient management of public affairs and delivery of services. In this quest, President Carter is likely to encounter the same persistent institutional obstacles to change his predecessors experienced.[27] For generations, Congress has been reluctant to destabilize existing relationships among executive branch agencies, clientele groups, and congressional committee empires.[28] Only if Congress, in a persevering reform wave, reorganizes itself institutionally in tandem with executive plans is any major restructuring likely to come about.

In posing these and many other issues before the 95th Congress, the success of presidential initiatives is more than usually uncertain. One might hazard a guess. Our limited acquaintance with Mr. Carter's style suggests that he is preeminently a cautious, prudent person. Unless we totally misconceive him, his characteristic approach to problems is gradualist, incrementalist, unencumbered by ideological rigidity or the manacles of political indebtedness. This just may be the prescription for cooperative fulfillment with the new Congress in the late 1970s.

State and Local Elections
Henry A. Plotkin

THE coattail effect has been part of the conventional wisdom about state and local results during presidential election years. The impact of the candidate at the top of the ticket on those farther down the ballot is traditionally seen as significant during national elections. One ancient political tale has a Brooklyn state legislator complaining to the local political boss about not seeing any signs of an active campaign being mounted on his behalf. The boss responds that a local politician during a presidential campaign is like the garbage in the Hudson River—drawn to the shore by the motion of a tugboat! In that particular election there was a happy outcome for the state legislator: the "tugboat" was Franklin Delano Roosevelt.[1] But by 1976 the coattails of the two major candidates were not all that long. Ticket-splitting had become more commonplace as the electorate felt less bound by party labels and more willing to divide its vote.

The results of the state and local elections in 1976 did little to change the enormous edge held by the Democrats in the nation's legislatures and governerships. Table 5.1 amply demonstrates the huge Democratic majority in the states.

The State Legislatures

In 1976, 43 states elected one or both houses of their legislatures.[2] The Democrats now control the legislature in 36 states. The shift in control of state legislatures was very slight. The Republicans

Table 5.1

State Legislative Election Results

State	Governor	Upper house	Lower house
Alabama	D	35 D	105 D
Alaska	R	12 D, 8 R	25 D, 15 R
Arizona	D	16 D, 14 R	23 D, 37 R
Arkansas	D	34 D, 1 R	96 D, 4 R
California	D	26 D, 14 R	57 D, 23 R
Colorado	D	17 D, 18 R *	30 D, 35 R
Connecticut	D	22 D, 14 R	93 D, 58 R
Delaware	R *	13 D, 8 R	25 D, 16 R
Florida	D	29 D, 10 R	92 D, 28 R
Georgia	D	52 D, 4 R	157 D, 23 R
Hawaii	D	18 D, 7 R	39 D, 12 R
Idaho	D	15 D, 20 R	22 D, 48 R
Illinois	R *	34 D, 25 R	91 D, 83 R
Indiana	R	28 D, 22 R *	48 D, 52 R *
Iowa	R	28 D, 22 R	60 D, 40 R
Kansas	R	19 D, 21 R	65 D, 60 R *
Kentucky	D	30 D, 8 R	78 D, 22 R
Louisiana	D	38 D, 1 R	101 D, 4 R
Maine	Ind	12 D, 21 R	89 D, 62 R
Maryland	D	39 D, 8 R	126 D, 15 R
Massachusetts	D	33 D, 7 R	194 D, 43 R
Michigan	R	24 D, 14 R	68 D, 42 R
Minnesota	D	49 D, 18 R	104 D, 30 R
Mississippi	D	50 D, 2 R	118 D, 3 R
Missouri	D *	24 D, 10 R	115 D, 48 R
Montana	D	25 D, 25 R	67 D, 33 R
Nebraska	D	Nonpartisan	—
Nevada	D	17 D, 3 R	35 D, 5 R
New Hampshire	R	12 D, 12 R	179 D, 221 R
New Jersey	D	29 D, 10 R	49 D, 31 R
New Mexico	D	33 D, 9 R	48 D, 22 R
New York	D	25 D, 35 R	90 D, 60 R
North Carolina	D *	46 D, 4 R	114 D, 6 R
North Dakota	D	18 D, 32 R	52 D, 48 R *
Ohio	R	21 D, 12 R	62 D, 37 R
Oklahoma	D	39 D, 9 R	79 D, 22 R
Oregon	D	24 D, 6 R	37 D, 23 R
Pennsylvania	D	31 D, 19 R	118 D, 85 R
Rhode Island	D	45 D, 5 R	83 D, 17 R
South Carolina	R	43 D, 3 R	112 D, 12 R
South Dakota	D	10 D, 25 R *	22 D, 48 R
Tennessee	D	23 D, 9 R	66 D, 32 R
Texas	D	28 D, 3 R	132 D, 18 R

Table 5.1 (continued)

State	Governor	Upper house	Lower house
Utah	D	17 D, 12 R	36 D, 39 R *
Vermont	R *	9 D, 21 R	77 D, 72 R *
Virginia	R	35 D, 5 R	78 D, 17 R
Washington	D *	31 D, 18 R	62 D, 36 R
West Virginia	D *	29 D, 5 R	90 D, 9 R
Wisconsin	D	23 D, 10 R	66 D, 33 R
Wyoming	D	12 D, 18 R	30 D, 31 R

* Switched party control.

SOURCE: *Congressional Quarterly Weekly Report* 34 (13 November 1976): 3162.

picked up the lower houses in Indiana, Utah, and Colorado (they managed a tie in Montana) and the state senates in South Dakota and Montana. The Democrats achieved a majority in the lower houses of Kansas and North Dakota and the senate in Indiana.

In general the Democrats did somewhat better than the Republicans in races for seats in state legislatures. Overall the Democrats achieved gains in 42 of the 83 contested houses; the Republicans increased their number in only 26.[3] In parts of the country, most notably the South, the Republicans failed to recapture the seats they lost in the sweeping 1974 Democratic victory. The inability to gain any ground in the South probably has the most serious consequences for the Republicans. One of the Republican party's major goals was to achieve a foothold in the formerly solid Democratic South and make those states politically competitive. Their failure to achieve this goal along with Carter's sweep of the South allows these states, at least temporarily, to remain in the camp of the Democrats. This is in sharp contrast to the belief held by many experts that a party realignment was taking place that would move the South increasingly into the Republican party.

Gubernatorial Results

In 1976 gubernatorial elections were held in 14 states, and the Democrats managed to increase their number of governors from 36 to 37. This represents the highest total of state houses held by any party since 1938. Democrats won nine of the fourteen elections while the Republicans won five (see table 5.2).[4] In seven states

Table 5.2
*Gubernatorial Elections of 1976*_____

State	Winner	Opponent
	Vote total (%)	*Vote total (%)*
Arkansas	David Pryor (D) * 594,722 (83)	Leon Griffith (R) 122,495 (17)
Delaware	Pierre S. (Pete) Dupont (R) ** 130,566 (58)	Sherman W. Tibbitt (D) * 97,514 (42)
Illinois	James R. Thompson (R) ** 2,963,247 (65)	Michael J. Howlett (D) 1,580,769 (35)
Indiana	Otis R. Bowen (R) * 1,219,380 (57)	Larry Conrad (D) 918,986 (43)
Missouri	Joseph P. Teasdale (D) ** 959,812 (50)	Christopher S. Bond (R) * 947,603 (50)
Montana	Thomas L. Judge (D) * 192,145 (63)	Robert Woodahl (R) 113,051 (37)
New Hampshire	Medrim Thompson (R) * 197,033 (58)	Harry V. Spanos (D) 144,504 (42)
North Carolina	James B. Hunt (D) ** 1,078, 068 (65)	David T. Flaherty (R) 562,442 (34)
North Dakota	Arthur D. Link (D) * 151,446 (51)	Richard Elkin (R) 137,392 (49)
Rhode Island	J. Joseph Garrahy (D) 221,770 (55)	James L. Taft, Jr. (R) 172,252 (45)
Utah	Scott M. Matheson (D) 277,875 (53)	Vernon B. Romney (R) 245,368 (46)
Vermont	Richard Snelling (R) ** 96,312 (53)	Stella Hackell (D) 74,087 (41)
Washington	Dixy Lee Ray (D) ** 732,697 (54)	John Spellman (R) 602,990 (43)
West Virginia	John D. Rockefeller IV (D) ** 489,949 (66)	Cecil H. Underwood (R) 251,754 (34)

* Incumbent.
** Party control switched.

SOURCE: *Congressional Quarterly Weekly Report* 34 (6 November 1976):
3147–54.

there was a change in the party of the governor. Delaware, Illinois, and Vermont replaced Democrats with Republicans; Missouri, North Carolina, Washington, and West Virginia did the reverse. Five incumbents were returned to office, and nine new governors, including one woman, Dixy Lee Ray of Washington, were elected. Most of the races for governor turned out as predicted, but there were some interesting results.

Perhaps the only race that could be called an upset occurred in Missouri where Democrat Joseph P. Teasdale defeated Republican incumbent Christopher S. Bond. Bond had been elected during the Nixon landslide in 1972 by a margin of 200,000 votes. His victory was helped substantially by Nixon's wide margin over McGovern. Missouri had not had a Republican governor since the Second World War, so the Teasdale victory in 1976 was not all that surprising. Still, many prognosticators had picked Bond to win the race because of his effectiveness in reforming state government. He accomplished this by working skillfully with Missouri's dominantly Democratic legislature. Nevertheless, as Missouri went for Carter by nearly 67,000 votes, this undoubtedly helped Teasdale squeak through with a 12,000-vote majority.

The gubernatorial race in Illinois was also of interest. Republican James R. Thompson trounced Michael J. Howlett, the chosen candidate of Chicago's late Mayor Richard Daley, by one of the largest margins in the state's history. Thompson's victory by nearly 1.4 million votes was an astounding feat and probably contributed heavily to Carter's loss to Ford by 100,000 votes. Howlett was clearly seen as a "Daley man." Indeed, the main issue that Thompson stressed during the campaign was that Howlett was merely a "puppet" of the Chicago mayor. Howlett did manage to carry Chicago by 65 percent, but he lost just about everywhere else.

Thompson's victory in Illinois could make him a rising star within the Republican party. The size of his electoral majority coupled with the death of Mayor Daley provide him with an opportunity to establish a solid record as governor. At forty years of age, his relative youth along with the fact that he is only one of twelve Republican governors will project him into the national spotlight. Thompson will be forced to run again in 1978 as Illinois moves the contest for governor out of the presidential year. But it seems unlikely that Illinois Democrats will be able to regroup in the wake of Daley's death to mount a serious campaign against Thompson.

The election of John D. Rockefeller IV in West Virginia adds another potential national figure to the Democratic party. Rockefeller trounced former Republican Governor Cecil H. Underwood by nearly 240,000 votes, which in West Virginia is almost a 2–1 margin. Rockefeller spent an estimated $2.7 million in the primary and general election, of which $2 million was his own money. This translates into approximately five dollars a vote. Rockefeller ran unsuccessfully for governor four years ago, on a vaguely populist platform emphasizing women's rights, gun control, and the war in Vietnam. In 1976 Rockefeller shifted tactics, emphasizing his ability as an administrator and financial manager. His victory in West Virginia makes him a significant figure in future Democratic national politics.

The only woman to win statewide office was Democrat Dixy Lee Ray of Washington. Ray, sixty-two years old, defeated her Republican rival, John Spellman, by a margin of 55 percent to 45 percent, and joined Democrat Ella T. Grasso of Connecticut as the only two women governors in the United States. Ray is a marine biologist and a former chairman of the Atomic Energy Commission; her main campaign plank was advocacy of nuclear power plants. She was an engaging campaigner. What makes her victory even more impressive is that it occurred despite Carter's loss of Washington by nearly 45,000 votes. At Ray's age, however, she is unlikely to become a serious national candidate. And although she was the only woman who won statewide office in 1976, her victory is probably more important for what it reveals about the public's attitude toward nuclear energy than as a sign of the salience of women in politics. She did not run a campaign that targeted women as a special voting bloc; she won on other issues. Perhaps her substantial victory demonstrates that the electorate is growing more sophisticated about candidates and cares more about issues than gender.

Public Issues

In a sense, the vote on the various ballot questions gives a clearer idea of what the public is thinking about specific issues than does the vote for individual candidates. This is true because candidates must take stands on many issues, and it is frequently difficult to determine which specific issue the voter considers most important. When the electorate votes on public issues on its state's ballot, it has the option of saying yes or no on that question, thus giving a very accurate reading of opinion on that single proposal.

The most interesting initiatives on the ballot in 1976 were those involving the use of nuclear power. In six states—Arizona, Colorado, Montana, Ohio, Oregon, and Washington— questions on the ballot called for the regulation of the growth of nuclear power plants.[5] In all six states, proposals for regulation were resoundingly defeated. The closest race was in Oregon where the nuclear regulation proposal lost by nearly a 3–2 margin. The most overwhelming defeat was in Colorado where it lost by nearly 2.5 to 1. These defeats, coupled with an earlier loss in California during the June primary, represent a substantial setback for environmentalists, who have taken up the anti-nuclear banner in recent years.

While it is difficult to determine the impact of this vote, it is certainly clear that the public is concerned about the energy question and willing to take some risks to ensure a plentiful supply of cheap sources of power. When the results were in, the Sierra Club argued that the utilities industry spent at least $6 million to defeat these initiatives and that the vote was less reflective of the public's opinion than the ability of money to influence an election. The pro-nuclear groups hailed these referenda as proof of the public's support for more nuclear power plants. Carl Walske, president of the Atomic Industrial Forum, asserted: "Twenty percent of the United States population has had an opportunity this year to vote on the need for nuclear energy, and they have affirmed it by a 2–1 landslide." [6]

Walske saw the vote as a clear endorsement for building more nuclear power plants and felt that policy makers in Washington should recognize this fact. Whatever the meaning of the vote, the public is obviously growing less enamored of the position taken by environmentalists on questions involving energy. This probably reflects the public's growing concern with the state of the economy and the increased dependence of the United States on foreign oil. The extent to which the pro-nuclear power advocates have been able to link their cause with questions involving jobs and national security definitely contributed to their success.

One of the more intriguing questions on a state ballot was the one involving the legalization of casino gambling in New Jersey. By a substantial margin, New Jersey voters endorsed a constitutional amendment to establish gambling casinos in the resort town of Atlantic City. This amendment would permit the state to regulate private gaming casinos in that economically beleaguered city. This approval represents a reversal of a 1974 vote in which the electorate turned down a proposal to legalize state-controlled casinos throughout the state. The reasons for the switch in voter preference probably include the more limited nature of this proposal—it involves only one city in the state—and the fact that casino advocates promised that they would raise additional revenues for the state. The latter reason was especially persuasive as New Jersey voters were still angry about the recently passed state income tax.

The significance of the New Jersey vote on gambling will be far reaching. On one level it reflects an increasing unwillingness on the part of the public to pay more taxes; to the extent that legalized gambling can defray state costs, it is likely to receive public support. The victory of the casino advocates is also attributable to the amount of money (estimated at $2 million) they spent in the campaign and the fact that the opposition was not nearly as well organized as it had been in 1974. The most important implication of this vote, however, will be the degree to which other states feel compelled to follow New Jersey's lead. Declining resort areas in Pennsylvania's Pocono Mountains and New York's Catskill region will increase pressure to legalize gambling in those areas. Mayors of large cities will likely use the Atlantic City precedent to argue that their areas need the revenue from legalized gambling. The net result of New Jersey's support of gambling may be a rapid spread of casinos throughout the Northeast in much the same way as New Hampshire's successful lottery influenced other states to offer similar games of chance.

The issue of gambling came up in other states as well. New York City voters endorsed "Las Vegas" nights for churches and other charitable organizations. Both Colorado and Vermont voters endorsed state lotteries. On the losing side, California turned down greyhound racing, Delaware rejected a proposal to legalize slot machines, and Detroit passed up the opportunity to have an advisory vote on casino gambling.[7] These states seemed to be bucking a national trend toward the use of legalized gambling to raise tax revenues. Indeed, it appears that as public confidence in government declines, the readiness to seek ways of raising revenue without more taxes increases.

In all, the 1976 election saw 330 issues on the ballot in 41 states.[8] Aside from questions involving nuclear power and gambling, there were only a few issues of note. The Maine and Michigan votes for mandatory deposit proposals were seen as a blow to the beverage industry, which opposed the concept of returnable bottles for economic reasons. In Massachusetts voters rejected a statewide ban on handguns by more than two to one. Voters in Michigan, Utah, and Montana rejected proposals to limit their states' budgets, while voters in Florida defeated an amendment to the state's constitution that would have limited the number of full-time state employees to 1 percent of the state's population. This last series of votes seemed somewhat to contradict the notion that the electorate was in an antigovernment mood.

State elections give interesting insights into the public's thinking on some key issues, but it is difficult to assess any long-term trends. Certainly the elections of Rockefeller in West Virginia and Thompson in Illinois place two new and attractive faces on the national political scene, but it is a hazardous enterprise to predict what their futures might be. If anything, the surprise nomination of Jimmy Carter should warn all political pundits of the dangers of assuming much about which personalities are likely to dominate American politics in the future. So much conventional wisdom about the electorate's opinion and mood seems to have gone by the board in recent years that only the most modest projections now seem justified.

The Outlook
for the Carter
Administration
Ross K. Baker

THE infant science of Carterology is rich in theory but poor in data. Even the conventional wisdom is remarkably inpoverished. A considerable amount is known about Carter the man, but much of what can be predicted about Carter the President must be inferred from campaign statements and reconstructed from his single term as governor of Georgia—not an impressive factual base on which to build a projection of a Presidency.

Abrupt discontinuities and breathtaking changes in a mature political system such as the United States are difficult to envision. The fundamental nature of the relationships among the various elements of American government are not likely to change. A neo-Jacksonian social upheaval and a major alteration of economic relationships seem similarly improbable. For example, there are differences not only in degree but also in kind between stating, as Carter did in his acceptance speech, that "it's time for a complete overhaul of our income tax system" and a revolution in taxation that fundamentally alters social and economic relationships. Determined and driven though Carter may be, he is no radical, and no one reading the results of the election can find evidence for a mandate for vast changes.

The constraints within which Carter must operate are those that would limit the freedom of any President—a daunting thicket composed of elements of Carter's electoral coalition, organized citizen groups, a wary Congress with a new and untried leadership, a bureaucracy prepared to defend its prerogatives, a web of entitlements including veteran's benefits and social security, a press that has come to view Presidents as less and less awesome, a network of international relationships and alliances premised upon continuity and constancy, a citizenry equally divided over whether unemployment or inflation is the principal economic peril, and an array of public policy matters over which any President simply has little exclusive control. Carter's innovations will be expressed most swiftly and surely in those areas in which his authority is most unchallenged; they will be more tentative and uncertain the deeper he ventures into the well-defended terrain of rival institutions and entrenched interests. The areas most susceptible to presidential control tend to be the most formalistic and symbolic. To borrow an agricultural metaphor (which may be apposite in discussing the prospects of an ex-farmer), this is the topsoil of personnel that may be readily plowed, fertilized, and otherwise rearranged. The subsoil of programs and policies is more resistant to the presidential plow. Below that is the refractory bedrock of institutions, interests, and coalitional imperatives where the forces are geological rather than horticultural.

In evaluating the prospects for the Carter administration we first examine those actions that the new President can take most readily. These are the symbolic gestures that telegraph to the American people the bona fides of the new administration. The nature of appointments, too, is replete with messages about the course the government will follow because the men and women who command the most prominent agencies of government presumably are compatible with the policies that President Carter wants to pursue.

We next look at the individual policies that the Carter White House seems likely to initiate or continue and the specific programs that flow from them. Economic policies and programs in social welfare, defense and foreign affairs, and government operations are those scrutinized most closely; they are the areas on which Carter placed the greatest emphasis in his presidential campaign.

We also examine the network of political and institutional relationships that comprise the constant elements of any President's tenure. In this realm are the President's relationships with Congress; with the major interest groups in the private sector, such as the business community and organized labor; with certain ethnic groups and the various elements that make up the political coalition of the Democratic party that won in November 1976.

Finally, we evaluate Carter's style as it has emerged thus far and examine his strengths and speculate on possible sources of difficulty for the new President.

Symbols and Selections: Some Carter Auguries

Part of Jimmy Carter's success as a candidate in 1976 was his novelty. He tenaciously stuck to Georgia rather than Washington, D.C., as his political command center. In a year in which discontent with government became an issue, his decision to play the role of outsider paid off handsomely. He deigned to carry his own luggage —or did so, at least, when photographers were present. He ran as a centrist when experts predicted that the primaries were tailor-made for ideologues. He redefined the nature of what constituted a political issue by successfully invoking the fundamental question of the relationship between the state and its citizens and went so far as to alter the conception of what it meant to be a Democrat.

Carter did not enter Washington in unseemly haste to claim his conquest. He lingered at Plains and on St. Simon's Island while his lieutenants supervised the transition of governments. His pace in making appointments was deliberate, if not downright leisurely. This gave substance to the notion that his personnel decisions were informed and judicious. He remained aloof from the early struggles for power among his subordinates, and in a manner strongly reminiscent of Franklin Roosevelt, waited until the victor emerged.[1]

One of his first announcements was that his nine-year-old daughter, Amy, would attend a public school in Washington. At a time when many citizens had become cynical about the feelings of politicians on school integration, the decision by the President-elect to send his daughter to school in a predominantly black district could find favor among black and white alike. This gesture demonstrated a measure of commitment to integrated education that could be invoked at a later date. Black Americans could be reassured that integration was a personal, rather than a rhetorical, commitment for Carter. Carter's long walk down chilly Pennsylvania Avenue from the Capitol to the White House on the day of his inauguration was a hopeful sign that the barriers between the President and the people would be less formidable.

Reassurance was also a dominant theme in Carter's earliest appointments. The nomination of Georgia banker Bert Lance as director of the Office of Management and Budget was widely interpreted as a signal to the American business community that basic tax and spending priorities would be guided by a levelheaded business executive rather than someone inimical to the interests of American industry.

Similarly, the designation of Cyrus Vance as secretary of state conveyed a message of continuity in foreign policy to the allies of this country, to the communist world, and to the American people. Unlike Henry Kissinger, who conducted American diplomacy within a well-developed theoretical framework, Vance is regarded as a negotiator and technician whose career has been that of trouble-shooter rather than theoretician. The Vance appointment also soothed the fears of those concerned that Carter, in the interests of redeeming his campaign pledge to place "outsiders" in positions of authority, would repose foreign policy in inexperienced hands.

OFFICIAL AND UNOFFICIAL FAMILIES

Cabinet appointments are dramatic harbingers of the future course of presidential policies. "As executive decisions go, they are preeminently concrete and visible. Among the earliest of presidential moves, they are treated as symbolic acts of considerable significance." [2] Despite the acknowledged symbolic and indicative value of these early decisions on the President's official family, those men and women who comprise his unofficial family, the White House staff, are of equal or even greater importance because ". . . the Cabinet does not represent many of the more recent enlargements of federal power and responsibilities," and "there are large vacuums in the Cabinet organization, and the President's staff has had to fill those vacuums." [3]

Carter showed a strong loyalty to people who had been with him since the beginning of his political career and a disposition to surround himself with trusted and familiar advisers as he began his Presidency. He wasted little time in designating his campaign press secretary, Jody Powell, as his presidential press secretary; and long-time aide and campaign manager, Hamilton Jordan, played a dominant role in Carter's search for executive talent during the transition. Old believers such as Powell and Jordan as well as Carter's campaign treasurer, Robert Lipshutz, his political director, Landon Butler, and his campaign issues coordinator, Stuart Eizenstat, will be in the inner circle. Even Carter's old friend Charles Kirbo, who has elected to remain with his law practice in Atlanta, will be available for instant consultation. Few members of the Carter cabinet will be able to approach the proximity to Carter that these individuals have achieved.[4]

Given the uncommon closeness of Carter to his old political associates and in light of the fact that "the members of the 'official family' of the Cabinet have stayed political dependents . . . devoid of constitutional or personal power," [5] the outlook for constructive relations between Carter and his cabinet must be guarded. The chances for a strong and coherent policy role for the cabinet will depend, in large measure, on Carter's success in reorganizing the federal executive branch. The formal jurisdiction of cabinet departments is often unrelated to the nature of the problems and challenges that the President must confront. A reorganization that would bring formal authority more into line with issues of public policy as they actually exist would almost necessarily improve the standing of the cabinet. But even if Carter should achieve a thoroughgoing reorganization, this alone would probably not be sufficient to make the cabinet preeminent over the White House staff. It is simply easier to develop policies with old friends and loyal associates than with department heads divided in their loyalties and attention between the President, Congress, and the powerful client groups who see cabinet officers as their spokesmen and instruments.

Should Carter's goal of a restructured executive branch be realized, Carter would be in a better position than any recent President to arrest the secular decline in cabinet effectiveness that has continued since the time of Andrew Jackson. Carter's formal statements indicated that he would take the cabinet seriously as a policy-making institution, and his meticulous process of choosing nominees seemed to reinforce this disposition.

Carter said in an interview shortly after his election that he intended to appoint "strong individuals" to his cabinet. He expected cabinet officers to take charge of their own departments rather than have them be run from the White House. The strength or ability of the cabinet chosen provides less of a clue about the ultimate effectiveness of the "official family" than the manner in which the President uses such talent.

Historically, the relations between Presidents and their cabinets have varied widely. Warren Harding, a resolutely mediocre President, vowed that he would fill his cabinet with the "best minds." He did recruit a few first-rate minds, but he failed to provide them with much direction. Whatever quality there was, was squandered by Harding's passive and diffident nature. The cabinet of Franklin Roosevelt was composed of "strong individuals" too, but Roosevelt went on to do whatever he chose and stood aside while cabinet members mauled one another. Of our recent Presidents, perhaps Truman was most able to approximate the criteria set down by Carter. He avoided being overwhelmed by the cabinet, as Harding had been, and did not allow them to neutralize themselves, as Roosevelt had done. Truman was quite willing to delegate responsibility to cabinet members and spoke with pride about the fact that

> I would ask the Cabinet to share their counsel with me, even encouraging disagreement and argument to sharpen up the different points of view. On major issues I would frequently ask them to vote and I expected the Cabinet officers to be frank and candid in expressing their opinions to me. At the same time, I insisted that they keep me informed of the major activities of their departments in order to make sure that they supported the policy once I made a decision.[6]

This would seem to be the "strong President–strong Cabinet" model that Carter would like to approximate. Statements made by Carter in the course of the campaign that he would select "outsiders" for his principal administration posts gave way in the aftermath of the election to the appointment of some prominent figures from past Democratic administrations and widely recognized business people and officials.

The decision to abandon an administration of political virgins may reflect the realization that in a modern, complex society it is virtually impossible to have attained any level of distinction without having been "contaminated" by the federal government or powerful institutions. For lower-echelon positions and non-cabinet advisers, Carter may well draw on younger people with no extensive experience in federal government—there is even a sprinkling of relative unknowns in the cabinet—but that is a long way from suggesting that cabinet members will not reflect, or be responsive to, the powerful interests that comprise the executive department constituencies. As Fenno has pointed out, ". . . The President's influence over the Cabinet member becomes splintered and eroded as the member begins to respond to political forces not presidential in origin. From the beginnings of his involvement in the appointive process, the President's power is subject to the pervasive limitations of the pluralistic system in which he seeks to furnish political leadership." [7] However brave and optimistic Carter's view of the cabinet and however well he succeeds with reorganization, promise rather than fulfillment has been the fate of recent cabinets.

THE CARTER CABINET
The cabinet of Jimmy Carter and the complement of principal advisers consists of 15 men and 2 women, as detailed in table 6.1. Two of Carter's top nominees are black and two are women. Their average age is slightly more than 53 and only one—James Schlesinger, who was designated Special Assistant to the President for Energy Matters—has ever served in a presidential cabinet. His service had been with Presidents Nixon and Ford.

Carter's promise to enlist women and blacks has been technically fulfilled with the designations of U.N. Ambassador Andrew Young, Commerce Secretary Juanita Kreps, and Housing and Urban Development Secretary Patricia Harris—who is both female and black. It is a matter of debate just how many "new faces" were recruited and the extent to which this particular Carter promise was kept. Only Kreps and Labor Secretary Ray Marshall had no prior government service, but all were sufficiently prominent and experienced to reassure the American people that important public matters would be placed in capable hands.

It is a cabinet with few ideologues, although the philosophical center of gravity is mildly liberal. Past Democratic Presidents would have found such a group congenial, but many of the nominees would not have been out of place in a moderate Republican cabinet either. They were chosen for their technical skills, their personal compatibility with the President, and with due recognition to the factor of regional and social balance. Those with identifiable histories of activism are activists of a decidedly moderate stripe. None are out of touch with the major political, economic, or social issues, but there are also no "barnburners" or intransigent zealots.

If Carter chooses to be active in the areas of their jurisdiction,

Table 6.1

The Carter Administration———————————————————————

Position	Name	Age on taking office	Residence when nominated	Religion
President	Jimmy Carter	51	Georgia	Baptist
Vice-President	Walter F. Mondale	49	Minnesota	Presbyterian
Secretary of State	Cyrus R. Vance	59	New York	Episcopalian
Secretary of the Treasury	W. Michael Blumenthal	51	Michigan	Presbyterian
Secretary of Defense	Harold Brown	49	California	Jewish
Attorney-General	Griffin B. Bell	58	Georgia	Baptist
Secretary of the Interior	Cecil D. Andrus	45	Idaho	Lutheran
Secretary of Agriculture	Robert S. Bergland	48	Minnesota	Lutheran
Secretary of Commerce	Juanita M. Kreps	56	North Carolina	Episcopalian
Secretary of Labor	F. Ray Marshall	48	Texas	Protestant
Secretary of Health, Education, and Welfare	Joseph A. Califano	45	District of Columbia	Roman Catholic
Secretary of Housing and Urban Development	Patricia R. Harris	52	District of Columbia	Protestant
Secretary of Transportation	Brock Adams	50	Washington	Episcopalian

Occupation when nominated	Previous experience	Education
Businessman	Naval Officer, farmer, businessman, Governor of Georgia	B.S., U.S. Naval Academy Union College
Senior U.S. Senator from Minnesota	Lawyer, Attorney-General of Minnesota	B.A., Minnesota LL.B., Minnesota
Attorney	Secretary of the Army, Deputy Secretary of Defense	B.A., Yale LL.B., Yale
President, Bendix Corp.	Special U.S. Trade Negotiator, Deputy Asst. Secretary of State	B.A., California M.A., Princeton Ph.D., Princeton
President, California Inst. of Technology	Physicist, Secretary of the Air Force	B.S., Columbia Ph.D., Columbia
Attorney	Judge, 5th Circuit, U.S. Court of Appeals	B.A., Georgia Southwestern LL.B., Mercer
Governor of Idaho	Insurance Sales, State Senator	Attended Oregon State Univ.
U.S. Congressman, 7th District, Minnesota	Farmer, Regional Director, U.S. Dept. of Agriculture	Attended Univ. of Minnesota School of Agriculture
Vice-President, Duke University	Professor of Economics	A.B., Berea M.A., Duke Ph.D., Duke
Professor of Economics, Univ. of Texas	Economist, writer	B.A., Millsaps M.A., Louisiana State Ph.D., California
Attorney	Defense Dept. Legal Adviser, Adviser to Lyndon Johnson	B.A., Holy Cross LL.B., Harvard
Attorney	U.S. Ambassador, Dean of Howard Univ. School of Law	B.A., Howard LL.B., George Washington
U.S. Congressman, 7th District, Washington	U.S. Attorney for Western District of Washington	B.A., Washington LL.B., Harvard

Table 6.1 (continued)

Position	Name	Age on taking office	Residence when nominated	Religion
Director, Office of Management and Budget	T. Bertram Lance	45	Georgia	Methodist
United States Ambassador to the UN	Andrew J. Young, Jr.	44	Georgia	Congregational
Special Asst. to the Pres. for National Security Affairs	Zbigniew Brzezinski	48	New York	Roman Catholic
Director of Central Intelligence	Stansfield Turner	53	Illinois	Protestant
Special Assistant to the President for Energy Matters	James R. Schlesinger	48	Virginia	Lutheran
Chairman of the President's Council of Economic Advisers	Charles L. Schultze	52	District of Columbia	Roman Catholic

they will be instruments of activism. If Carter chooses a course of moderation and partial measures, they will underscore his moderation. Only a few of the nominations gave rise to much controversy. The designation of Griffin Bell for the post of Attorney-General was challenged by some black leaders who charged that as a federal judge he was unsympathetic to civil rights. Other black leaders rose to his defense. Patricia Harris was held to be unfamiliar with urban problems but was defended for her basic competence. All of Carter's original nominees gained confirmation except for Theodore Sorensen, who withdrew his name from consideration. Questions were raised about his use of government documents for private purposes.

It is not an ideal cabinet if that term is meant to imply absolute and unchallenged distinction in all areas. But some of Carter's optimal choices were unavailable, and the designation of others might have caused him political problems that could have hampered his

Occupation when nominated	Previous experience	Education
President, National Bank of Georgia	Highway Commissioner of State of Georgia, Banker	B.A., Georgia
U.S. Congressman, 5th District, Georgia	Minister, Church Executive, Civil Rights Leader	B.S., Howard B.D., Hartford Theological Seminary
Director, Research Institute on International Change, Columbia University	Director of the Trilateral Commission, Professor of Political Science	B.A., McGill Ph.D., Harvard
NATO Commander, Southern Europe	Admiral, U.S. Navy	B.S. U.S. Naval Academy M.A. Oxford
Professor of Economics	Chairman, Atomic Energy Commission, Director of Central Intelligence, Secretary of Defense	B.A., Harvard Ph.D., Harvard
Senior Fellow, The Brookings Institution	Director of the Budget under Lyndon Johnson	B.A., Georgetown Ph.D., Maryland

policies. It is far better for Carter to have intelligent and compatible individuals to assist him in the framing and implementation of his policies than intractable luminaries who might be inclined to substitute their best judgment for his. The President is answerable to the voters for the policies that he undertakes. He must provide coherence and direction for these policies. These necessary objectives are harmonious with the cabinet that he assembled and that cabinet is fully capable of meeting the challenge of enlarged or altered responsibilities.

Domestic Policies and Programs: Making Haste Slowly

In the course of his presidential campaign Jimmy Carter often told his audience that "it's time for a complete overhaul of our income tax system," or, "if you don't want to see the federal government reorganized, don't vote for me." He also pledged to cut the unemployment rate, hold down inflation, and produce a balanced budget by fiscal year 1981. He pledged himself wholeheartedly to a program of national health insurance and, somewhat less passionately, to the Humphrey-Hawkins full-employment bill, which sets a goal of reducing unemployment among adults to 3 percent within four years.

In the area of foreign policy he promised to withdraw American troops and nuclear weapons from Korea; deemphasize the importance of our relations with the great powers, giving primacy instead to those with our allies, and halt the spread of nuclear weapons. Although we do not hold Presidents strictly accountable for their campaign promises or demand that they adhere rigidly to the party platform on which they ran, these pledges often have been redeemed to a surprising degree and have attained partial fulfillment in many other instances.[8] Jimmy Carter can be expected to try to make good on his personal pledges and those that he wrote into the platform. The question is really not *whether* he will seek to fulfill them, but rather *how* and *in what order*. An examination of a few of the policies and programs to which Carter directed attention during the campaign would be useful in discerning the broader outlines of his approach to important areas of domestic and foreign concern.

THE ECONOMY

The economy confronts Jimmy Carter with an ineluctable problem and with a set of dilemmas incapable of easy resolution. Virtually every economic indicator tells him that the country is in a near-recessionary state. Unemployment stands at 8 percent; inflation, barely under control, could be unleashed with full fury once again. A particularly severe winter confronted Carter with serious problems of energy shortages and energy-related unemployment.

Classical liberal economic wisdom suggests that certain stimulative measures be taken to drive down the rate of unemployment. Typically, such measures would involve a tax cut or rebate of some kind, which infuses purchasing power into the economy; public works programs, which initiate projects in the public sector that would create jobs; and public service employment wherein the government provides jobs in new or existing areas. More indirectly, tax incentives for business can create new jobs by fostering the purchase of new equipment or expansion of factories; facilitating the acquisition of credit and increasing the supply of money encourage new housing construction and industrial expansion; or government can subsidize certain industries. From this partial inventory of stimulative techniques, it can be seen that remedies for a stagnant economy can be found in both the public and private sectors. There is an abundance of devices at a President's disposal for galvanizing a flagging economy.

The negative corollary to stimulation, however, is inflation. If unemployment is economic enemy number one for Carter, inflation is clearly the second most menacing problem. Stimulating the economy produces jobs. It can also produce a measure of inflation. Conservative economists and many businessmen believe that government spending that causes government indebtedness pits the public sector against the private sector for available money to borrow—a competition weighted in favor of government. This, the businessmen argue, inhibits the expansion of plants and the purchase of new equipment and results, ultimately, in unemployed workers. If government, then, by its efforts to reduce unemployment spends money and goes into debt, it bids up the price of money available for borrowing, which restricts the ability of industry to create jobs and inflates the cost of credit as well. This is an article of faith among many businessmen.

Carter has added his own stringent requirement to this frustrating and baffling complex of problems and that is his promise to present a balanced federal budget by fiscal year 1981. This objective clearly places important boundaries on the amount that the federal government can spend to revitalize the economy and reduce unemployment. Given these strictures, what is the general line of attack that Carter will take to provide jobs, inhibit inflation, and balance the budget?

What we will probably see is an economic high-wire act requiring unusual coordination. Stimulus will be provided, but it will probably combine private-sector incentives with direct governmental action—some combination of tax relief and public service or public works jobs. Incentives or outright subsidies will probably go to distressed industries such as construction, combined with some measure of tax relief in which the greatest benefits will accrue to lower-income groups where the need is greatest and the disposition to spend is strongest.

Decisions made to remedy unemployment will take cognizance of their effect on inflation. Planning toward the goal of a balanced budget several fiscal years down the road will be evaluated in light of its compatibility with an economic upturn. Assurances to labor on federal spending programs to foster unemployment will be set off against the need to reassure the business community that the capital investment by the private sector will not be inhibited. Increases in the gross national product that may be salutary in terms of achieving low unemployment will have to be compatible with controlling inflation. Pledges of assistance to hard-pressed minority groups cannot be read by the business community as a declaration of war on them.

The most obvious circuit-breaker on the upward trend of wages and prices would be wage-price controls, or at least a set of guidelines. Carter will want to try his skills as a "jawboner" before considering the more extreme measures. Outright controls have been ruled out, but voluntary wage-price guidelines seem to have found favor with some Carter advisers; others favor advance notice of price increases by industry. Carter's responsiveness to the concerns of environmental groups by moratoriums on construction of nuclear power plants may be neutralized by extensive mining and burning of coal for power. Controls on natural-gas prices may please consumers impoverished by high utility rates but may worsen shortages in the long run.

SOCIAL PROGRAMS

Carter also placed welfare reform high on his agenda. In quest of this goal, Carter should have strong support in Congress where the present welfare system has virtually no advocates. Carter has supported the principle of one more-or-less uniform nationwide payment adjusted to compensate for differential costs of living in various parts of the country and funded in substantial measure by the federal government. Carter's preference would seem to be the gradual introduction of such an approach and the consolidation of the food-stamp program in this essentially standardized welfare payment. Such a technique would unquestionably have the support of the mayors of the large cities and the governors of the most populous northern states. It would also be responsive to Carter's minority-group constituency and, depending on its cost, a Congress with little appetite for the present system.

Only slightly less urgent in terms of Carter's priorities is a comprehensive national health insurance program. Total national health costs now approach $120 billion annually. Despite estimates by the Social Security Administration that only 12 percent of the population has no health insurance under private or public plans, there are considerable disparities in coverage among those Americans who are insured, and national health insurance proponents have argued that universal coverage would achieve both standardization and control of the unchecked rise on costs.

Here again, as in the case of standardized national welfare payments, Carter has expressed himself in favor of a piecemeal attack, with coverage extended initially to such groups as the elderly, pregnant women, and children. If the program succeeded with these groups, it could be extended to the rest of the population. Another interim technique would involve a limited-benefits approach rather than experimental coverage of certain vulnerable sections of the population. This would entail coverage for "catastrophic" illnesses requiring long-term care.[9]

Foreign Policy

The foreign policy positions of the major parties have converged so decisively that there is a temptation to regard as trivial many of the putative differences cited by Ford and Carter during the election campaign. One is hard-pressed to formulate the archetypal "Democratic" or "Republican" positions on the Middle East, southern Africa, Eastern Europe, SALT, negotiations with Vietnam, or relations with our traditional allies. If the narrowness of the area of partisan disagreement required demonstration, there is the reality that the most heated foreign policy exchanges in the presidential debates took place over the issues of evaluation rather than policy.

Ford and Carter debated the extent to which the Soviet Union dominated Eastern Europe, the degree to which American prestige in the world had eroded, and the manner in which U.S. foreign policy expressed fundamental American morality. To be sure, Ford defended his foreign policy more resolutely than he did the Reagan-dictated terms of the Republican platform, and Carter's self-dictated foreign policy platform did not inhibit him greatly. Nonetheless, even personal differences over foreign policy were inconsequential.

Carter's foreign policy perspective is held to be deeply influenced by the concept of "trilateralism" set forth by Zbigniew Brzezinski.[10] This approach stresses collaboration among the United States,

Western Europe, and Japan to formulate policies for dealing with the developing world and deemphasizes the great-power policies of Henry Kissinger.[11]

The Strategic Arms Limitation Talks (SALT) negotiations, which Henry Kissinger described as 85 to 90 percent complete, may have to wait some time before the remaining issues are nailed down. Carter suggested during the campaign that his philosophy of SALT envisioned numerical reductions in the strategic weapons of the United States and the Soviet Union, rather than simple ceilings on certain missiles and bombers. This adds a novel element to SALT, which the Soviets will take some time to ponder. Carter may also be expected to press forward with his proposal for an outright five-year ban on underground nuclear testing for either military or peaceful purposes. Peaceful testing now occupies a special category; underground peaceful detonations up to 150 kilotons are permitted. Carter's appeal for a halt to all testing, which was issued on January 24, 1977, was one of his first acts as President.

NUCLEAR PROLIFERATION

Carter associates the question of general nuclear proliferation with the problem of restraint in weapons development, deployment, and testing among the superpowers. He has stated that pleas to less-developed nations to desist from developing nuclear capabilities have a hollow and unconvincing ring if the great powers show no restraint. This relationship was set forth with considerable force by Carter at a United Nations conference on May 15, 1976. This speech presently stands as the most elaborate expression of his view on any foreign policy issue. That he singled out nuclear curbs suggests that the Carter administration may attempt to make its boldest discretionary foreign moves in the area of nuclear nonproliferation and testing.

Among the proposals that might well emerge from the Carter administration are: (1) a moratorium on the sale of plutonium reprocessing plants until a more permanent set of controls can be imposed through international agreements; (2) a five-year ban on all underground nuclear testing; (3) reduction of strategic forces among the nuclear powers; and (4) a general international energy conference presumably under UN auspices, on the model of the food and population conferences of recent years.

These proposals could be folded into a general rubric of an

"Alliance for Survival" to dramatize the initiatives and mobilize support for them. Carter has set great store in his credentials as a nuclear engineer and has said that strategic arms limitations is a challenge to which he brings personal skill and understanding. His personal interest in nuclear problems would seem to argue for a major move in this direction.[12]

ENERGY AND INTERNATIONAL ECONOMICS

Of the most menacing international problems, two are in the area of international economics, but as in domestic policy, categorization is not neat. These problems, too, have military, domestic, economic, and alliance-relevant implications. The first, unquestionably, is the question of oil pricing by OPEC. The extent to which oil prices will rise has dire implications for the shaky economies of Britain, Italy, and the developing nations, but all nations will be affected to a degree. Nominal price increases of 5 to 10 percent would be vexatious. A larger rise could be cataclysmic. At his first press conference Carter uttered the moderate admonition that "I would hope that all the OPEC nations would be reticent about increasing the price of oil." So judicious a statement coming on the heels of Carter's combative stand on oil boycotts in the second debate with Ford may induce the OPEC oil ministers to be equally judicious in their future price increases.[13] Certainly the defection of Saudi Arabia and the United Arab Emirates from the substantial OPEC increase in December 1976 could be seen as a friendly gesture to Carter.

Closely related to OPEC decisions is the question of the U.S. role in shoring up the deteriorating British economy. Even if the International Monetary System undertakes an economic rescue operation, much of the cost will be borne by the United States. If the United States acts alone to assist Britain, Carter may be in the position of having to administer some harsh economic remedies to our traditional ally as a condition for American assistance. Substantial increases in the world price of oil would simultaneously limit what the United States could do for Britain and contribute to the further erosion of Britain's economic position.

CRISIS IN SOUTHERN AFRICA

Southern African policy is a legacy that Carter will inherit. Had the Geneva talks on Rhodesia between the white government of Ian

Smith and black nationalist leaders with Great Britain in the role of intermediary produced a quick and easy agreement on transition to majority rule, Kissinger would have had his last triumph. Carter would have been relieved of the problem of grappling with that particular strand of the southern Africa tangle. The long-range problem for Carter in Africa, however, is not Rhodesia but South Africa.

The United States has important political and economic ties to the Republic of South Africa. The strategic location of South Africa at the tip of the Cape of Good Hope makes it militarily important to the United States. American companies have invested more than $1 billion in South Africa, and many American corporations have subsidiaries there. Both South Africa and the United States have been concerned about Soviet sponsorship of national liberation movements in Angola, Mozambique, Rhodesia, and Southwest Africa (Namibia). The government of South Africa, however, has a long-established policy of racial separation and discrimination against its African population known as *apartheid*. The United States has been officially opposed to *apartheid*, but aside from imposing an arms embargo on South Africa and condemning the practice in the United Nations and in conversations with the South African leaders, this country has never really tried to get tough with South Africa and induce it to change its racial policy.

With its ties to the United States and its assistance of Henry Kissinger's peace initiative for Rhodesia, South Africa becomes an embarrassment for this country in its relationships with the black states of Africa and the entire developing world. If Brzezinski's concepts of trilateralism as an alternative to deepening enmity between the industrialized and nonindustrialized world are carried to their logical conclusion, the Western democracies will have to ponder their relationships with South Africa. The Carter administration may take the lead in this basic reassessment. It may do so not only because of the broad international implications of the problem of a white-ruled state on a black continent, but also because the American black community that supported Carter so enthusiastically is becoming increasingly impatient with American inaction.[14]

Carter can be expected to be much more vigorous than his predecessors in applying pressure to South Africa to reform its racial policies. Although Carter admitted that economic sanctions would be counterproductive, he may seek to work through the American business community to open up opportunities for black South Africans in American-owned facilities in that country. He may be more ready to align this country with the developing world in its censure of South Africa in the United Nations, or even reduce the level of Amerian diplomatic relations with Pretoria. Vigorous pressure of some kind on South Africa can certainly be anticipated.

THE MIDDLE EAST

Residual effects of last-minute gestures by the Ford administration may present Carter with problems in the Middle East. The decision by the United States to vote for a Security Council resolution criticizing Israel's administration of the territories occupied after the 1967 war temporarily chilled U.S.–Israeli relationships. The Israelis see the gesture as part of an American effort to retain a brokerage position in the Middle East. The Israelis are reluctant to undertake these negotiations before their national elections. Egypt's President Anwar Sadat is pressing to purchase American weapons and has hinted that he would turn to his old supplier, the Soviet Union, should Washington refuse his requests.

A number of foreign policy experts, including Brzezinski, have endorsed a plan in which the United States would declare that the proper boundaries for Israel would be its pre-1967 frontiers coupled with guarantees of Israel's security. The Geneva conference would be convened with these overall goals in mind, and among its participants would be the Soviet Union. Components of the overall settlement would be, presumably, the demilitarization of the Golan Heights, much of Sinai, the West Bank, and Gaza with a UN force stationed in those zones that could be removed only by the consent of all parties. Israeli withdrawal would be in phases, and the Arabs would agree to rescind boycotts and states of belligerency and recognize Israel de jure. It could conceivably include a West Bank Palestinian state, which seems to have gained more favor even among Palestinians.[15]

Whatever long-term merits such a policy would have, it is unlikely that Carter would seek to press it on the Israelis so soon after his election and so soon before theirs. Although relations between the United States and Israel will eventually resume their normally cordial nature, Carter will probably want to make gestures of friendship to reassure the Israelis that the November vote in the

Security Council was just a mean-spirited parting shot by Henry Kissinger. Carter may also want to sell Egypt more arms. President Sadat made a favorable impression on a visiting group of American senators and congressmen; and Congress, which has asserted the power to veto arms sales, might be willing to allow military sales to Egypt to take place rather than force Sadat back into the arms of the Soviet Union.

Although Carter may have more leisure in foreign policy matters, his overseas honeymoon cannot be expected to last very long. The possibility of renewed turmoil in southern Africa, an OPEC increase in oil prices, shaky and hesitant moves toward democracy in the Iberian peninsula, edgy allies in Japan and Korea, a footloose President Sadat and a wary Israeli government make Carter's foreign agenda urgent, if not implacable.

Executive Branch Reorganization

In the strictest sense, the reorganization of the federal executive branch is neither a program nor a policy but rather a structural reform. Nonetheless, the ability of the Carter administration to achieve its objectives in substantive policy areas and its success with individual programs depends, in large measure, on administrative effectiveness. Reorganization, at the least, is a precondition for the revitalized cabinet that Carter envisions.

Efforts to restructure the federal bureaucracy can be traced back to Theodore Roosevelt's administration—and virtually every President since the first Roosevelt has tried his hand at reorganization. Because virtually all the agencies of the executive branch are established by statute, the President has been dependent on Congress to provide him with the authority to consolidate, abolish, or otherwise tamper with bureaucracies of its creation. Few agencies, moreover, are not favored by some important constituent group in the private sector, to say nothing of powerful chairmen of congressional committees who are loath to see Presidents trifling with bureaus that come under their jurisdiction.

These daunting obstacles to wholesale reorganization have led one veteran of the reorganization wars to warn that "the investment of political capital is so great and the risk of loss so substantial that a President can at best achieve one or two major reorganizations during his years in office—if he selects his targets shrewdly." [16]

As governor of Georgia, Carter requested that state's legislature to allow him to reorganize the executive branch. After a great deal of energetic arm-twisting, the authority was granted—by a single vote. Carter will probably have an easier time securing the statutory authority from Congress to reorganize. What is less clear is the *extent* to which they will allow him to reorganize. For although Congress has shown a willingness in the past to give Presidents the authority to reorganize, the interest groups that could bring their influence to bear at a national level are so much more formidable than those that could be mobilized at a state level that any estimate of success is impossible to make.

A far-reaching reorganization could disrupt the long-standing triangular relationships among legislators, interests, and bureaucrats. Carter's plan to preside over a "purposeful, manageable, and competent government" could well be ambushed by powerful committee chairmen in Congress, wary and resourceful bureaucrats, and lobbyists of powerful interests who prefer the status quo, however inefficient and self-defeating it may be.[17]

Reformers in the Senate were also on the move during the 94th Congress when the Select Committee of Committees headed by Senators Adlai Stevenson (D-Ill.) and Bill Brock (R-Tenn.) reported out a bill to realign the jurisdiction of Senate committees.[18]

The degree to which Senate committee realignment and executive branch reorganization succeed, if they succeed at all, will probably affect Carter's plans for reorganizing the bureaucracy over which he has most complete control—the White House staff. The structure and functions of the President's "unofficial family" are largely determined by his own style and preferences. He can work his will most effectively on those offices not established by congressional statute and to that extent, the organization consisting of "The President's Men" can be as vast or as streamlined as he chooses.

Carter has been so critical of the growth of governmental bureaucracy that he will likely make some effort to reduce the size of the White House staff. Under Presidents Nixon and Ford the White House staff ballooned to almost six hundred people. Carter will want to reduce this number substantially if for no other reason than to serve as an example for the rest of the executive branch and convince Congress that he is serious about reorganization. But clearly, the extent to which Carter feels disposed to make cuts will depend upon his success in restructuring cabinet-level departments, since at least part of the rationale of past Presidents in placing policy responsibility in White House staffs was provided by the haphazard organization of the major departments of government.

Relations with Congress

General pledges of cooperation with a new President, especially one of the same party as the congressional leadership, are to be expected. Beneath these pledges, however, some early hints of potential discord appeared on individual actions proposed or supported by Carter during the campaign. Carter's campaign pledge to reduce the defense budget $5 billion to $7 billion was greeted with skepticism by Congressman Les Aspin (D-Wis.). Ways and Means Chairman Ullman showed little enthusiasm for Carter's promise of a tax cut. Senator William Proxmire proclaimed the Humphrey-Hawkins bill that Carter had endorsed "in deep trouble" and cast doubt on its wisdom. These reservations were expressed well before Carter began his consultations with congressional leaders, however, and may be subject to revision when Carter's precise objectives are clarified. Congress is usually hard-pressed consistently to defy a determined President, but Carter will have to choose his targets carefully and not expend his credit with Congress on dramatic but controversial initiatives. The withdrawal of the Sorensen nomination further demonstrated the power of Congress.

The Congress is probably at the bottom of the list of those who owe any tangible obligation to Carter. If this is true of Congress in general, it is even truer of the grandees of the House and Senate, some of whom won reelection without significant opposition and did not benefit from Carter's scanty presidential coattails. On such matters as immediate steps to alleviate unemployment, welfare reform, and a mandatory national health-insurance system, there is substantial agreement between Carter and Congress. Others, such as tax reform and Carter's ambitious plans for government reorganization and a budgetary revolution known as "zero-based budgeting," contain the seeds of considerable dissonance between the two principal institutions on Pennsylvania Avenue. Even on those matters of general accord, the modes of implementation offer abundant prospects for wrangling.

It is difficult to estimate the prospects for success in Congress for any individual administration program or initiative, but with the overwhelming Democratic margins of 292–143 in the House and 62 to 38 in the Senate, a workable majority exists at least in a nominal sense.

Carter will find the congressional leadership accommodating but not servile. Speaker of the House Thomas P. ("Tip") O'Neill seems genuinely delighted with the prospect of working with a Democratic President and is doubly pleased by the choice of Representative Jim Wright (D-Tex.) as majority leader. Cordial relations between the Speaker and the majority leader augur well for a unified House leadership position on the President's legislative program.

Carter's experimental and incremental style will probably be congenial with that of Congress. His belief in lean and frugal government will be a natural favorite with cost-conscious senators and congressmen. His informality and understated manner will be welcomed by those on Capitol Hill who are leery of presidential highhandedness.

But Carter has few close friends and no cronies in Congress. Georgia's two senators, Herman Talmadge and Sam Nunn, endorsed his presidential aspirations at a relatively late date, and among non-Georgians in the Senate, only Joseph Biden (D-Del.) and Birch Bayh (D-Ind.) could be said to have declared for Carter well before his nomination became a certainty.

The "down-home connection" might be useful for Carter in establishing good relations with such important committee chairmen as Russell B. Long (D-La.), John L. McClellan (D-Ark.), John C. Stennis (D-Miss.), and James O. Eastland (D-Miss.) in the Senate. Dixie Democrats loom less imposingly in the House, but regional pride can be invoked there as well.

The basic elements are in place for a highly satisfactory relationship between Carter and Congress. Despite some skepticism on certain Carter programs, a few bruised egos left over from the campaign, and the fact that Carter is the first President since Eisenhower who has not risen through the legislative ranks, there is no reason to forecast discord between the White House and

Capitol Hill. Indeed, should serious strife occur, it would imply an extraordinary erosion of some very auspicious omens.

Supporters, Supplicants, and Satraps: Carter and the Interest Groups

Presidential victories are only partially the result of the individual qualities of the candidate, and the attainment of presidential goals are not solitary crusades. Coalitions of voters helped to produce Jimmy Carter's majority on November 3, 1976, and coalitions of interests will play a major role in the success of his plans in the four years that began on January 20, 1977. Groups and individuals make claims on Presidents whom they have supported, and each is prepared to demonstrate that his support was the deciding element. The payoffs demanded of a President by one group are often harmonious with those of other groups. The exactions of some claimants, however, conflict with those of other groups whose contributions were equally meritorious.

Carter cannot casually or arrogantly dismiss these claims. If he wishes a second term as President he will have to reassemble his electoral coalition in 1980. But even if he did not wish to extend his stewardship, he would need the help of powerful groups to support his policies for the next four years. It is also true that Carter could never fulfill his pledges and honor his obligations to the point of the absolute satisfaction of any single claimant. What he must avoid is the "zero-sum game," in which one constituency's benefit is seen as another's loss. He can please large-city mayors and unemployed blacks with essentially the same programs and approaches, but a decision to limit the use of nuclear power plants may please environmentalists and alienate consumers and members of the Building Trades Department of the AFL–CIO. He needed all to win and needs all to govern. How Carter can redeem his campaign pledges, maintain his electoral constituency, and enlist the support of major interests for his programs—all with limited resources—is one of his greatest challenges. But as President of all the people he must also make the determination of what is in the public interest and not restrict himself to dispensing rewards to the faithful and scourging the infidels. Jimmy Carter must also be regarded as legitimate in the eyes of the 39 million Ameri-

cans who did not vote for him while retaining the support of the
41 million who did.

ELECTORAL DEBT, POLITICAL CREDIT

No one yet knows the precise nature of Jimmy Carter's philosophy
of discharging political indebtedness. Several groups feel that they
have a unique or special claim on him. Scarcely a week elapsed
after the election when a number of them convened to submit their
due bills. Big-city mayors called a conference in Chicago demanding, among other things, emergency antirecession aid for cities,
the establishment of an urban bank to provide low-cost loans to
cities, the creation of more jobs for central-city residents, and the
consolidation of federal urban programs.[19]

Carter's long-standing pledge of access for mayors will surely be
fulfilled. The other items on the shopping list may be more elusive.
Mayors may find that Carter will gladly aid them in debt consolidation, which will cost the federal government nothing. They are
hopeful that he will press for the federalization of local costs of
welfare, which will relieve some of their burdens and provide some
measure of fiscal relief. But mayors who had come to feel like un-
wanted supplicants to the Nixon and Ford administrations may
regard Carter's half-loaf as tasty fare indeed.

Carter is said to owe a very special and personal debt to the black
voters of America, who gave him almost 90 percent of the 6.6
million votes that they cast. This extraordinary total represents not
only a political expression but a testament of faith as well. Black
Americans have some very definite expectations of Carter. Fore-
most among them is the belief that Carter will swiftly move to provide jobs for black workers. Unemployment among black workers
currently stands at 13.5 percent—almost double the overall rate.
Fiscal stimuli such as tax cuts do little to provide jobs for blacks
because deficiencies in skills and education preclude them from
getting desirable jobs even in an expanding economy. The job-
retraining programs and vocational training efforts of the past have
been costly and so lengthy that the jobs were filled before the
trainees could complete their instruction.

General economic stimuli will, of course, provide some relief.
Programs for the revitalization of the cities will also be helpful to
urban blacks. Assistance to the depressed housing industry will be
an additional source of jobs, especially if the unions in the con-

struction trades are induced to hire blacks as craftsmen and apprentices. General benefits have always trickled down to blacks to some extent. But more is needed, and more is expected. Carter knows this and will probably target some of his stimulative measures on housing rehabilitation and educational improvements in inner-city areas. He may provide inducements to industry to create jobs in the cities, or even act to open suburban housing to blacks since the greatest growth of employment opportunities has been in the suburbs. Carter will probably defend such specialized programs for blacks not only in terms of equity but also because it is economical and efficient to focus remedies on those sectors suffering the most. Controversial proposals such as abolishing the federal minimum-wage law in order to reduce unemployment among black teen-agers will probably be avoided. Although this suggestion may make sense in terms of teen-age unemployment, it is unacceptable to organized labor.

Organized labor, speaking through George Meany, president of the AFL–CIO, was not specific and exacting in its claims. Meany modestly requested an open door and a friendly ear at the White House. He will certainly get this, as well as a hearing on such labor "musts" as a bill to facilitate picketing at construction sites and repeal of the authority for state right-to-work laws.

But not all of Carter's decisions will be so simple, nor the choices he confronts so pure. Increasingly, decisions that appear to reside at first glance squarely in one functional area have repercussions in others. Decisions on defense spending exemplify this problem. Whatever merits the B-1 may have as a replacement for the aging B-52 bomber, a decision to move from development to deployment or to halt such a process becomes, simultaneously, a decision on further indebtedness as opposed to a balanced budget. It evolves as a choice between continued work for aerospace workers and widespread sectoral unemployment. It also becomes a tradeoff between détente and continued international tensions. It is also expressed as an agenda-setting quandary as to whether social programs or defense should receive priority.

It may be expected that if Carter can limit his payoffs to symbolic appointments, increased access, deference, sympathy, and costless reorganizations, consolidations, and improvements in efficiency, these will be the preferred methods of political debt-service. But not all of Carter's choices will be so painless, and even fewer can be accomplished unilaterally.

Nevertheless, Jimmy Carter has shown himself a master of nuance. Skillfully crafted ambiguity and unusual subtlety in his statements gives him a great deal of flexibility and room for maneuver. Carter's position on Vietnam amnesties offers a good example of this. During the presidential campaign he promised that one of his first acts as President would be to issue a proclamation of amnesty for draft resisters. He seemed to leave the door open for broader amnesties to Vietnam-era deserters. In December 1976 groups favoring the inclusion of deserters met to urge Carter to encompass deserters in his amnesty. This was followed by a letter from one hundred congressmen asking him to reconsider issuing any amnesties. Having thus been bracketed by the most radical expressions on both sides of the issue, Carter proclaimed himself in favor of his original moderate position. Operating in such a manner, Carter protects himself from promising too much but allows his political creditors to satisfy themselves with claims of total victory when they have achieved only partial success. Carter can then share in the credit and use it as evidence that he keeps his promises.

THE CARTER STYLE

A pattern seems to emerge from what Carter has said and what others predict about him across a wide range of issues. It may be summed up in the words "phasing," "degree," "calibration," and "targeting." Carter has made pledges to achieve a variety of objectives—tax reform, controlling military costs, welfare reform, national health insurance, overseas troop deployments, and governmental reorganization. It seems to reflect a genuine desire to redeem all these campaign pledges but a strong disposition to proceed with caution, discernment, and experimentation. His inclination to grant a tax cut or rebate is qualified by his belief that it is best directed at lower-income groups. His desire to restrain defense costs is essentially an argument for greater efficiencies rather than a reduction in the dollar amount in the defense budget or even a reduction in the rate of increase in military costs. His approach to welfare reform envisages a period of transition from the old system to a new one rather than abrupt change. His national health-insurance goals are contingent on the success of more limited trials. His pledge to withdraw troops from Korea will likely occur in phases, if he makes that move. His promise of reorganization may proceed in stages, not only to placate a wary Congress, but also to test the waters, evaluate tentative results, and build a case for more far-reaching changes.

Carter's technique is to proclaim general objectives and ask for time to work out the details and study the problem. He can then settle back and allow the opposing forces to assemble their arguments and make their representations to him. Typically, this is done either by interested parties or by staff members who happen to be on opposite sides of the issue. This provides Carter with both extreme positions and some notion of the middle ground. He can then begin to formulate his approach and estimate how far he can safely proceed. It is a technique Hegelian in method, Aristotelian in result, and from all reports, Carterian to the core.

Carter may also have the capacity to wrap radical initiatives in innocuous packages. The nomination of W. Michael Blumenthal, an executive of the Bendix Corporation, for the post of secretary of the treasury can be seen as a gesture to the business community. Blumenthal, however, is an experienced economist who is said to favor comprehensive national economic planning. This is an unusual view for a corporate executive to hold. If an academic economist with similar beliefs had been nominated for the Treasury post, the business community would probably have regarded it as a hostile appointment. Carter is, in short, the very model of the complete incrementalist, the readily recognizable American half-a-loaf politician who has some personal vision of a better tomorrow but a healthy political awareness of the concrete realities of today.

Perils and Pitfalls

It is probably premature to speak about clouds on the horizon of the new administration, when the horizon itself is so dimly seen. Nonetheless, some potential sources of discord can be discerned. Some of these possible points of friction could be found in any Presidency, some tend to bedevil Democratic Presidents more than Republicans, and some may be inherent in the particular kind of man Carter seems to be and the kind of administration that he has assembled.

OLD BELIEVERS AND PARVENUES
One very bold prediction can be made concerning the relationships between the original corps of Carter true believers and those who

joined the Carter forces after his nomination seemed assured: in any showdown between the old believers and the parvenues, the old believers will probably gain the upper hand. The farther back one goes with Carter, the greater will be the likelihood that one's position will be unassailable. The old believers are wary of people whom they regard as opportunists. Their loyalty to Carter is intensely personal, and their proximity to him will be jealously guarded. Carter reciprocates this loyalty with an intense fidelity to those who believed in him in the face of a skeptical world. The skeptics may be converted, but they are admitted only grudgingly to the priesthood and stand the greatest risk of being defrocked.

Loyalty of this kind produces cohesion, a common vision and direction, and reduces discord in the inner circle. Old believers such as Jody Powell and Hamilton Jordan always prided themselves on their ability to admonish Governor Carter when they thought he was wrong. Whether their powers of admonishment with President Carter will be equally strong is another matter. Personal loyalty of this intensity also produces a frame of mind that sees conflicts in terms of "us" versus "them." It also paves the way for "mind-guarding" and "groupthink" whereby Presidents are shielded from unpleasant realities and dissonant opinions and the maintenance of group cohesion becomes an end in itself.[20]

Such unswerving mutual loyalty can be a shelter for the incompetent and knavish if a President's commitment to an individual, by dint of his long and faithful service to the President, transcends necessary judgments about the individual's ability to perform effectively and honorably. It is hoped that the most egregious examples of this kind of shortsightedness are sufficiently fresh in the minds of the President and his aides that they will be shunned.

EXPECTATIONS AND PERFORMANCE

One peril that Carter may encounter is the fact that expectations are running high among a number of groups that look upon the Carter administration as an oasis after eight years of wandering in the Nixon-Ford wilderness. For these, the clarion call for major changes sounded during the campaign tended to obscure the many elaborations and qualifications that were later supplied by the candidate. The public is not galvanized by subtleties nor are winning coalitions built with qualified and conditional statements. But even if Carter has not yet delineated his transcendent vision, the simple fact that he is a Democrat, who ran on a platform consonant with Democratic platforms of the past, inevitably raises expectations.

For some, the benefits anticipated from the new administration are tangible and personal. The one thousand résumés a day that flowed into the Carter transition office in Washington in November and December of 1976 testify eloquently to the fact that whatever symbolic benefits government may be said to provide, concrete payoffs yield infinitely greater satisfaction. But with scarcely more than two thousand patronage positions to dispense in Washington, Carter may be led, as Lincoln was, to observe that for every ten people seeking a single job, you get nine enemies and one ingrate.

There will be blacks who are disturbed by what they see as an insufficient number of black officeholders. Feminists may accuse Carter of reneging on his commitment to women. Labor leaders may be disturbed at the economic conservatism of some Treasury appointees, and businessmen may regard the Justice Department as a den of antitrust zealots. Journalists may find in the appointment of recognizable figures from past administrations, or people associated with powerful institutions, a betrayal of Carter's promise to appoint new faces. Wary bureaucrats may resent the callowness and inexperience of the political appointees leading them.

BLUNDER ON THE LEFT?

The Carter administration will be more pragmatic than doctrinaire. Carter's tendency to "pair" advisers during the campaign—to draw simultaneously on the counsel of the "hawkish" Paul Nitze and the "dovish" Paul Warnke and to seek the counsel of both George Wallace and Andrew Young—suggests that he has set up a kind of ideological counterpoint. There may well be a tendency to see issues in terms of "tradeoffs" and "equality *versus* efficiency" choices. We may see a cohort of disenchanted people falling away from Carter during the shakedown period. Clashes between Carter and prominent liberals and activists may be written off as personality conflicts, but they suggest possible problems with the left wing of his party, whose acceptance of Carter has always been grudging. Activist disillusionment with Carter came to the surface spectacularly when consumer-advocate Ralph Nader accused Carter of reneging on a promise to clear cabinet appointments with him. It would seem inappropriate to have a President's entire cabinet approved by a single unelected individual. Nevertheless, the mere assertion of such a right portends a stormy relationship between Carter and professional reformers such as Nader and John Gardner of the "citizens' lobby" Common Cause, whose expectations of Carter may be the most thoroughly unrealistic.

Numerically, the liberal wing of the party is not dominant; but it is articulate, sensitive to slights, and requires extensive care and feeding. Lyndon Johnson learned to his sorrow the price of scorning liberals, and although an issue of the magnitude of Vietnam will probably not arise to plague Carter, liberal sharpshooters can inflict painful wounds. Carter is fortunate in this regard, in having a certifiable liberal hero as his vice-president.

WHERE FRITZ FITS

The essential accuracy of Nelson Rockefeller's characterization of the vice-president as "standby equipment" is difficult to challenge. Attitudes toward the vice-presidency have changed from the days when Mr. Dooley could observe that "everybody runs away from a nomination for Vice-President as if it was an indictment by the grand jury." Nonetheless, the ardor with which American politicians now court the second highest office in the land often turns into a case of unrequited love. Let us turn, finally, to the man in quest of a mission and then to the man in whom the fulfillment of that mission resides.

One must always be very skeptical of what Presidents promise for their vice-presidents. Even with the best intentions, Presidents seem unable to vest their vice-presidents with authority more satisfying than designating them the official American mourner at funerals of foreign chiefs of state. Gerald Ford appointed Nelson Rockefeller, with a grand flourish, to preside over a moribund Domestic Council. John Kennedy believed that ex-Senate Majority Leader Lyndon Johnson could be his nuncio to the Congress, but when Johnson advanced himself as leader of the Democratic caucus, he was rebuffed by his old colleagues and found himself presiding over the Equal Employment Opportunities Commission and giving out ballpoint pens in West Berlin.[21]

To use the President of the Senate for White House congressional liaison raises questions both of propriety and separation of powers. Perhaps a more appropriate liaison function is that of emissary to the liberal wing of the party—a role that Mondale is said to have performed exceedingly well during the campaign. There is peril here for Mondale, which should be acknowledged, and that is whether he can simultaneously advocate liberal positions to Carter and sell Carter's positions to liberals. Any evaluation of Carter's plans for Mondale must be held in abeyance until the results are in. If Mondale looms large in the Carter administration, the President will have made a signal contribution to institution building that would not be the most insignificant achievement of his incumbency. If ever a vice-president were equipped to step into an expanded role, it is Mondale.

THE CARTER CHARACTER

As we face the four years of the administration of Jimmy Carter, we have behind us a landscape strewn with the wreckage of defunct, discredited, and rejected Presidencies. The 1976 election seems to have stamped Gerald Ford as a necessary but ineffectual caretaker. Watergate transformed Richard Nixon into an embittered recluse. Vietnam made Johnson into a vengeful and self-pitying lame-duck President who gloried in the defeat of his beloved party. Does Jimmy Carter have the qualities to succeed in his first term, win reelection, and leave the White House in 1984 with his dignity and self-esteem intact?

The most comprehensive approach to the psychology of the Presidency is that provided by James David Barber in *The Presidential Character*.[22] At the conclusion of his study Barber recapitulates the qualities he sees in the most desirable presidential type, what Barber calls the "active-positive" President. "Their approach," he writes, "is experimental rather than deductive, which allows them to try something else when an experiment fails to pan out, rather than escalate the rhetoric or pursue the villains responsible. Flexibility in style and a world view containing a variety of probabilities are congruent with a character ready for trial and error and furnish the imagination with a wide range of alternatives."

The few straws in the wind that we can grasp seem to tell us that Carter comes very close to at least that one attribute of the most successful presidential paradigm. The final words of Barber's study written in the early 1970s may well have been written for Jimmy Carter, though the author could not have foreseen his emergence in American politics. If our primitive hunches about Carter are correct, they could be words of uncommon prescience: "A Presidential character who can see beyond tomorrow—and smile—might yet lead us out of the wilderness." [23] The smile has come to define the outward expression of Carter's personality. It is the vision that has yet to be fully revealed.

7

The Meaning of the Election
Wilson Carey McWilliams

OR almost a hundred years," V. O. Key wrote in 1952, "catastrophe has fixed the grand outlines of the partisan division among American voters." [1] Key had two disasters in mind: the Civil War, which created a solidly Democratic South; and the Great Depression, which established the Democrats as the party of working-class and low-income voters. After all the turbulence of the last quarter century, it seemed to be that traditional coalition that elected Jimmy Carter in 1976.

On closer analysis, however, the election of 1976 shows that the old battle lines, though still very persistent, are changing and yielding to more contemporary divisions. This, I will argue, is especially evident in (1) the role of the South in the 1976 election, (2) Carter's relative weakness in northern industrial states, and (3) the increased salience of the "social issue" in electoral politics.

I will also contend that all these aspects of the 1976 election are symptomatic of deeper challenges to American democracy. In the pattern of the 1976 campaign, in fact, there is more than a hint that a new period of soul-searching and trauma, if not "catastrophe," may await America. Certainly, the election of 1976 promises a changing and uncertain future for American party politics.

The Election

THE SOUTH

The Democratic South, the product of Key's first catastrophe, seemed to have passed into history before this year's election. Carter won more southern states than any Democratic candidate since World War II. Disaffected by Democratic support for racial integration and disdain for "states' rights," traditional southern Democrats had experimented with third parties in 1948 and 1968 and, in increasing numbers, had turned to the Republican party. Republicans were encouraged to hope that a presumably conservative South would form a reliable part of a "new Republican majority." Carter's near-sweep of the South was a terrible setback for this Republican "southern strategy." [2]

The election of 1976, however, did not represent a return to traditional southern Democracy. Carter carried a new South, decisively different from the "Solid South" that grew out of slavery, the Civil War, and Reconstruction.

In the first place, the traditional southern electorate was white, and Carter won only a minority of southern white voters. His victories depended on overwhelming black majorities and were possible only because the Voting Rights Acts of the 1960s had made it possible for previously disenfranchised blacks to register and vote.

Nevertheless, the sizable white minority that supported Carter was also crucial to his victory. It also points to major changes in the South. After all, blacks had voted in the South before, especially during Reconstruction. Then, however, southern whites voted with near unanimity to establish "white supremacy" and exclude blacks from political power. Blacks continued to vote down to the turn of the century, when fear of a coalition between radical populist whites and black voters helped to inspire the whole apparatus of laws designed to exclude black and poorer white voters from any effective suffrage. Many lower-class southern whites had, in effect, voted to disenfranchise themselves rather than endanger the edifice of "white supremacy." [3]

Architects of the "new Republican majority" always overestimated the conservatism of the white South. V. O. Key observed time and again that southern voters were, if anything, a bit more liberal on economic questions than voters elsewhere. As had been true in the 1890s, however, such liberal or radical economic attitudes tended to be checked, balanced, or outweighed by the desire to preserve a segregated and white-dominated society. Racism, not conservatism, was the key to the "southern strategy." Long before, Key had argued that only an "orgy of race hatred" could produce a Republican South.[4]

In the civil rights era, racial animosity certainly came to the surface. Violence was frequent, and something like an "orgy of race hatred" did develop. Even so, Lyndon Johnson lost only the Deep South states to Goldwater, and in 1968 many southerners preferred Wallace to Nixon. Nixon swept the South in 1972, but that was a national as well as a regional pattern. The violence and the hostility of the 1950s and '60s was not enough, in other words, to create a Republican South despite southern bitterness toward the Democratic party.

At the same time, more and more southern whites have accepted the end of segregation, at least as a fait accompli. Always, in the South, there had been courageous critics of the established order, and other southern whites had opposed segregation privately but kept silent from diplomacy or fear. Many southern whites, too, had defended segregation because it was traditional, "the southern way of life," even though they doubted or rejected the racial theories used to justify the system. For this last group, segregation was often an embarrassment, and after a token resistance for "the honor of the flag," they were glad to see it go. Finally, even strong supporters of the old order found many reasons to be reconciled to its passing. Nightmarish visions of anarchy and rapine did not materialize. In fact, the South entered into a period of economic dynamism. When racial violence erupted in northern cities, shattering northern self-righteousness, the white South felt less uniquely stigmatized and even began a mild self-congratulation about how well—in comparison to the North—the South was managing the change in race relations. Increasingly, racism disappeared as an explicit concern of *public* policy, whatever people's private views and conduct.

This does not mean that southern whites, any more than their northern counterparts, have become racially enlightened. It does mean that southern whites do not reject—and are growing accustomed to—political cooperation with blacks. Excluding blacks from the political system is no longer a real option, even if whites desired it, and consequently, appeals to "white solidarity" are relatively pointless. In the new political environment, "race issues" will continue to be important, but they will follow, rather than determine, the lines of party politics. In this respect, the South is simply becoming like the rest of the country.

Many southern white voters, of course, would not have voted Democratic if the candidate had not been a southerner. In the South, Carter benefited from the estrangement between the South and the country as a whole. The peculiar history of the South, beginning with slavery, has helped make southerners a "conscious minority." [5] And, in its turn, the rest of the country regards the South as culturally retarded. For a great many Americans, a southern accent is, prima facie, evidence of ignorance, and southern institutions—like the Southern Baptist church—are considered quaint at best and probably backward. The gentlemanly "Rebs" of the old Westerns have yielded to slack-jawed, often malevolent "country boys," but stereotyped "southerners" still frequent the media. Lyndon Johnson wrote that he hesitated to run in 1964 because he doubted that a southern President could unite the country.

> I was not thinking just of the derisive articles about my style, my clothes, my manner, my accent and my family—although I admit I received enough of that kind of treatment in my first few months as President to last a lifetime. I was also thinking of . . . a disdain for the South that seems to be woven into the fabric of Northern experience. . . . Perhaps someday new understanding will cause this bias to disappear from our national life. I hope so, but it is with us still. [6]

Feeling scorned and resenting indignity, southerners have been inclined, like any minority, to defend their own.

Southern resentment and defensiveness are not limited to whites. To be sure, southern whites often consoled themselves for the humiliations they suffered at northern hands by inflicting worse injuries on blacks. But southern blacks *also* suffered from the prejudice against things southern, since their culture and institutions have been decisively shaped by the southern experience. In fact, since most black Americans have their cultural roots in the South, they are also affected. It seems likely, in fact, that once assured that Carter's belief in racial equality was genuine, many blacks voted for Carter *because* he was southern.

As the novelty of a southern President wears off, Carter and the

Democrats may lose some of their new margin of strength in the region. Certainly Republican strategists hope this will be the case. But it seems equally likely that 1976 was a "critical election," marking the conscious emergence of a postsegregation South, economically confident and eager for national recognition.[7] Jimmy Carter, a peanut farmer and a "born-again" Christian, was ideally suited to be the symbol of a South risen again. Possibly, as has been true at every juncture in recent American politics, the Democrats have come up on the right side of a critical election, identifying themselves with the feelings and aspirations of a people ready to make their claim for civic equality and dignity. The election of 1976, in other words, may have added a normal southern majority to the Democratic coalition.

Familiarity, in any case, will add to Carter's strength in the North. All of his southern qualities emphasized, to northern voters, that Carter was an outsider and an unknown quantity. Urban Catholics and Jews suspected his evangelical Protestantism. The disastrous *Playboy* interview seems to have been intended to allay liberal fears that Carter might advocate censorship or other moralistic legislation. His mannerliness, too, seemed excessive to voters who wanted him to voice their indignation. This sort of anxiety and suspicion will almost certainly dissipate as the country becomes accustomed to Carter and his style. But the fact that it existed in 1976 illumined another dimension of contemporary American politics.

THE ELECTION AND THE ECONOMY

No principle of recent political analysis has been more firmly enshrined than the belief that high unemployment rates portend a Democratic landslide. Since the Great Depression, the Democrats have been regarded as the party of labor and associated with government intervention to reduce unemployment. Time and again, voters have declared that they trust the Democrats to run the economy more than they trust Republicans. In economic affairs, Americans tend to see the GOP as inept and hostile, the party of business ranged against the interests of "the little guy." Republicans have virtually conceded the point, seeking to counter this Democratic advantage by arguing—as both President Ford and Senator Dole did in 1976—that Democrats produced full employment in the past only by leading the country into war. It is not a very sound argument, although it is sometimes persuasive, but the attempt to categorize the Democrats as the "war party" is some indication of Republican despair whenever the election turns on economic issues alone.

By that standard, 1976 should have been a Democratic triumph in all the industrial states. Unemployment rates were higher than they had been since the depression and they had been high during the whole Nixon-Ford term. The administration trumpeted a "recovery" that barely dented those alarming figures. Already able to run against Nixon and Watergate, the Democrats were also able to run against Hoover and the depression.

In the congressional election, something like a Democratic landslide did develop. Democrats held the gains they had made in the "Watergate election" of 1974, retaining many seats once regarded as safely Republican. In the presidential election, however, Gerald Ford did very well in states where unemployment might have been expected to hurt him badly. Even where Carter won, his margins were closer than expected, and Ford carried two states in the deeply depressed industrial Northeast (New Jersey and Connecticut), dominated the industrial Midwest, and swept the Far West.

A more familiar, less culturally alien Democrat—Edward Kennedy, for example—might have won a number of states where critical blocs of voters, alarmed by Carter's strangeness, voted for "the devil we know." Certainly the Ford campaign made excellent use of the Presidency to emphasize the tried-and-true safety of their candidate. Nevertheless, the fact that normally Democratic voters would defect to Ford despite the ramshackle condition of the economy says a good deal about the decline of the feelings and loyalties that grew out of the Great Depression.

Voters who preferred Ford were likely to worry about inflation and taxes more than they feared unemployment. And politically, it is the *fear* of unemployment that matters; even in the worst periods, only a fraction of the labor force is actually unemployed.

Traditionally, it took very few layoffs to make almost all workers uneasy and anxious about their jobs. Before the New Deal and the rise of organized labor, the decision to hire and fire was an employer's prerogative. Senior and highly paid workers, who had the most to lose, had reason to fear that they would "get the sack" in difficult times. Skill was sometimes a source of security, but as Marx had observed, industrial technology tended to displace skilled workers in favor of unskilled, less expensive labor. Unemployment was close to an ultimate calamity since few workers had any resources other than their jobs, and almost no one felt safe once layoffs began.

Now, many workers feel reasonably secure despite high rates of unemployment. A large number of workers feel that their jobs are protected by seniority rights, job tenure, or other provisions of agreements between employers and employees. Both collective bargaining and bureaucracy tend to protect senior employees against arbitrary firings and make it much easier, if layoffs are necessary, for employers to discharge new employees—who are disproportionately young, poor, and nonwhite. The "two-tiered economy" exists inside the bureau or the factory.

Unemployment is still a real danger, of course, even for relatively protected workers. Such workers are, however, insulated against short-term economic fluctuations. Unemployment becomes a relatively distant worry, not to be compared with immediate problems like paying the bills out of a paycheck depleted by taxes and shrunk by inflation. Workers who feel shielded against unemployment are likely to demand that unions win cost-of-living increases even if, in hard times, this means unemployment among the newly hired. And similarly, workers who are nearing retirement worry less about teen-age unemployment than they do about the impact of inflation on their pension funds.

These relatively privileged workers are part of the "contract society," a growing mass of Americans—ranging from secure organized labor to upper-middle-class professionals—whose position depends on statutes and contracts as much as skill, and who are exempted from the logic of the market. Their advantages derive from the organized power of interest groups and collective agents, and they rely on public authority to support or actively promote their private interests (for example, through licensing laws that allow professionals to control the supply of labor). Most members of the contract society feel secure barring a major social upheaval, and it is no surprise if they shy away from uncertainty and distrust change.

None of this is new. Social theorists have been describing this evolving pattern for a good many years.[8] Nearly a quarter-century ago, Samuel Lubell suggested that this sort of development might lead erstwhile Democrats into the Republican party.[9] Lubell erred in stressing interest too much and memory too little. Workers who had entered the work force in or before the 1930s' depression, and those who grew up during the depression years, remembered the old economy with its omnipresent threat of unemployment— and the memory colored their reaction to changes in the unemployment rate. Now, the old economy seems very distant if people remember it at all. Members of the contract society are increasingly inclined toward fiscal conservatism. They do not want to pay higher taxes; they distrust "big spenders"; they are suspicious of bureaucracy. After a few missteps, Carter responded to this current of opinion, emphasizing his own concern for fiscal restraint and a balanced budget. In general, members of the contract society must be persuaded to support change. They own shares in the ship, and are not eager to rock the boat.

This turn of mind provides Republicans with a great opportunity to win converts from the Democratic majority, but it is an opportunity that will probably go unused. Although the members of the contract society have conservative tendencies, they want to conserve the America created by the New Deal. Few Americans, Archie Bunker aside, believe that we could "use a man like Herbert Hoover again." The Republican insistence on speaking the language of economic individualism, assailing "big labor" and defending "the private sector" does not attract the "children of the New Deal" whose position presumes an active, protective government and who see organized labor as at least a vital part of American society.[10]

During the campaign, President Ford—like Nixon in 1972— found it necessary to play down his party and to praise Democratic leaders like Harry Truman. But it is doubtful that admiration for Truman—now something of a vogue—would lead many Republican leaders to advocate the Fair Deal in Republican primaries. The Republican right, the survival of another era in American politics, makes it all but impossible for the Republicans to change in the direction of the electorate. Conservative southerners were once a problem for the Democrats, but after Roosevelt they never had a decisive voice or veto in party councils. The Republican right, by contrast, has grown stronger with time, as President Ford learned in 1976. On the basis of the past record, Republicans will miss their chance to win the economic confidence of the American center, and Democrats will continue to enjoy the allegiance of workers in the contract society as well as those outside it who are most vulnerable to unemployment.[11]

THE SOCIAL ISSUE

In recent years, the "social issue" has been an important Republican asset.[12] In 1968, concern about crime and civil disorder led many voters to desert the Democrats. Similarly, in 1972, McGovern's positions on abortion, marijuana, and an amnesty for deserters and draft evaders were generally considered to have hurt him among traditional Democrats.

Carter's relative social conservatism lessened the impact of such issues in 1976. Some voters probably defected to Ford because Carter did not support an antiabortion amendment to the Constitution. Others may have been offended that Carter proposed to pardon draft evaders, although the Appalachian region—militantly hostile to amnesty in 1972—was a Carter stronghold. Since Carter insisted that a pardon, unlike an amnesty, presumes the *wrongness* of the acts being forgiven, he disarmed many potential critics. Thus, candidate choice in this year was not closely related to alternative positions on the general "social issue."

But the 1976 election was almost unique in the intrusive attention devoted to the private lives and personal beliefs of the candidates. Inevitably, after the Watergate scandal, candidates were expected to be persons of unquestioned probity. This year, however, candidates were subjected to a scrutiny that went far beyond a concern for personal integrity. Carter felt compelled to discuss his code of sexual behavior. Mrs. Ford discussed premarital sex and marijuana, as did Mrs. Carter, and the candidates' children commented, with apparent frankness, on their parents' ideas. Neither candidate, probably, gained many converts because of these performances, although the *Playboy* interview undoubtedly hurt Carter. It is more notable that such questions should be asked and answered. Until quite recently, it would have been assumed that presidential candidates held traditional beliefs about private morality and, in the unlikely event that they held differing views, would not offend the electorate by saying so. In any case, such matters were *private*, not appropriate subjects for public prying and discussion, and a reporter who raised them openly would have been seen as intolerably impertinent.

Obviously, in 1976 candidates and voters alike considered that "private" moral beliefs *had* become public issues. Part of this, undoubtedly, was due to Watergate. Raised in the belief that the checks and balances of the Constitution made it a self-regulating mechanism that radically reduced our dependence on public virtue and enlightened statesmen, Americans were shaken by the crisis. The Constitution weathered the storm, but a less inept usurper than Mr. Nixon might have survived, and the whole affair emphasized how much contemporary America *does* depend on the President's character and virtue.

Moreover, for some years, "private" issues have been forcing their way into public places. Racial discrimination in private clubs —not to mention private corporations and trade unions—has been a matter of public concern for some time. The women's movement has made sex roles into political questions. Life-style issues such as hair length and sexual preference have troubled great public institutions like the army.[13] Republicans have tended to gain most from the introduction of these issues. Divided between voters who adhere to traditional beliefs and advocates of new social patterns and moral standards, Democrats have learned to tread warily. Comments hostile to homosexuals are thought to have damaged Senator Henry Jackson's campaign in the 1976 New York primary, but any *other* statement would have weakened the senator's hold on his traditional working-class supporters. Senator McGovern was helped in the primaries in 1972 by the very "social" positions that helped derail his campaign in the general election. But although Democrats have suffered most, Republicans have not gone unscathed. It certainly did Republicans no good, for example, when President Nixon—so sententious in public—was revealed to be extremely foul-mouthed in private. Voters were bound to suspect at least, that Republican moral professions were only hypocrisies.

All politicians and parties have been buffeted by the intrusion of traditionally private issues into public realms. In fact, the "social issue" reflects a changing idea of the very *meaning* of politics and political life in America.[14]

The Meaning

THE ELECTION AND THE AMERICAN TRADITION

Political theorists point out that our definition of politics shapes our fundamental ideas about political things. Traditionally, Americans have regarded the meaning of politics as self-evident, needing no explanation. As in so many things, Americans accepted the political ideas that we had received from the Framers. In recent years, however, American complacency has been shaken; the election of 1976 may be a sign that it has been shattered, and the American political tradition itself has become an issue.

The "science of politics" on which the Framers based the Constitution presumed that politics should not concern itself with the fundamentals of morality. The Framers believed that human beings were naturally free, self-preserving, and self-seeking and that they created government for limited purposes, ceding some "natural rights" and retaining others. First, government existed to protect citizens against each other and against outsiders; second, it was intended to help them in their quest for power and for mastery over nature. Government was needed to restrain vice and advance interests. It was not the job of government to shape human character and moral personality. That task was reserved for "society," the private world of families, churches, and communities. In Thomas Paine's famous definition,

> Society is produced by our wants and government by our wickedness; the former promotes our happiness *positively* by uniting our affections, the latter *negatively* by restraining our vices.[15]

However, the Framers worried, given their concern to protect individual freedom, that the emotional hold of local communities would be too strong, restricting liberty and retarding progress. And in part, the Framers simply took the existence of strong families, churches, and communities for granted. In any case, they gave most of their attention to "freeing" the individual from excessive social control, even though this involved undermining the position and prerogatives of society.

But even the Framers did not doubt that government depended on and could support social institutions. Governments had the right to safeguard the "health, morals and safety" of their citizens. Within their jurisdictions, governments could define and protect marriage, assign authority over children and regulate their education. They could define life and the right to take it. And through taxation and the regulation of commerce, they could shape the world of work, property and exchange. The line between state and society was far from absolute, and the character of government depended on the "wisdom and firmness" of the people.

Some leaders of the early Republic went a good deal beyond the

Framers in this respect. "Statesmen," John Adams wrote, "may plan and speculate for Liberty, but it is Religion and Morality alone, which can establish the Principles upon which Freedom can securely stand. . . . The only foundation of a free Constitution is pure Virtue." [16] Moreover, despite considerable diversity, the "private order" of families, churches, and communities spoke in terms of a common teaching. Human beings, in that traditional creed, were naturally dependent, social, and political animals. They needed the common life to develop emotional security, moral faculties, and personal identity. Individualism and self-seeking ran contrary to human nature rightly understood; self-mastery and self-knowledge were essential elements of true freedom, and what was "naturally right" mattered more than "natural rights." It was that substantive tradition which Alexis de Tocqueville had in mind when he argued that free institutions in America were maintained more by American customs than by American laws.[17]

In the past, Americans found their emotional security and learned their substantive beliefs in the private order. There they found the social and moral security that made it possible to accept the uncertainties of a public universe characterized by individualism, conflict, and change. Individual freedom was the tip of the iceberg; the real foundation was provided by the traditional creeds that set limits to freedom and that defined the uses to which freedom should be put. "Our constitution," Adams declared, "was made only for a moral and religious people. It is wholly inadequate to the government of any other." [18]

CONTEMPORARY CHALLENGES

In 1976, Americans were painfully aware that the traditional teachings were fading and that the social and moral "givens" of the past were under attack where they survived at all. Rather consistently, the private order has been weakened and undermined in American history; now it approaches collapse. A national economy made local communities and governments less important, and almost impotent, in dealing with the vital economic sphere of life. Unable to rely on locality, Americans have been encouraged by increasing mobility—especially in the age of the automobile—to move in response to economic currents, breaking their ties with friends and family. In the pain of leaving and being left, we learn to minimize our commitments to new friends and homes.

Too, organizations that are large enough to be effective in advancing our interests tend to be so large that we are dwarfed, and we withdraw into private spheres where we have the sense that we matter. The media, however, pursue us into our most intimate retreats, entering the home and probing for the deepest corners of the mind. Local beliefs and cultures lose autonomy and control. More and more, we feel isolated in a world of mass and change that we can neither understand nor control, and in which we are hard-pressed to maintain any psychological or moral autonomy. A growing number of Americans simply drift in the social current, relating to others only through style and image, making few deep commitments, finding little intimacy and less meaning.

Americans doubt the stability and continuity of ultimate retreats like the family. Changing sex roles threaten traditional family patterns. Established moral codes are publicly defied and ridiculed. Inevitably, many Americans are driven to ask whether they can "count on" enough to make it worthwhile to sacrifice for the future. Perfect security, of course, is impossible: blacksmiths once thought they had a stable trade. But if citizens are to make any commitments at all, they need the sense that some things are relatively predictable, stable, and continuing. Even if we think of law and morals as no more than "rules of the game," it ought to be obvious that if the rules change in the middle of the game, people will wonder if it makes sense to "play fair." We should not be surprised if more and more Americans are inclined to "take care of number one." Early in the nineteenth century, Alexis de Tocqueville commented that democratic individualism makes

> every man forget his ancestors . . . hides his descendents, and separates his contemporaries from him; it throws him back for ever upon himself alone, and threatens in the end to confine him entirely within the solitude of his own heart.[19]

These tendencies alarm Americans even as they reflect and adjust to them. It has become a popular truth in our time that when freedom is reduced to "just another word for nothing left to lose," people will wish to abandon or escape from freedom. Public and political freedom depends on private and personal security, which makes it necessary to attempt to rebuild the links between citizens and generations, strengthening social ties, local communities and the "art of association" that Tocqueville regarded as vital to the future of democracy. Concern about the social issue, however inarticulately and incompletely, is based on a recognition of the need to restore the civic bond.

This is no longer a private problem. As recent politics suggests, issues such as sex roles, the structure and duties of the family, and the limits and powers of local communities have become public questions in which action by public authority is critical. Dominated by the liberal belief in the separation of state and society, government has paid little attention to rebuilding or reconstructing the private order. Rather, it has allowed and even encouraged social fragmentation.[20] The record of local communities in the past has certainly been bad enough to merit watchfulness—the old South is example enough—and bureaucratic corporations are hardly "voluntary organizations" in the old image of society. But the sins of the old private order and the defects of contemporary social life do not argue for a world *without* moral foundations or social security; they strengthen the case for reconstruction.

POLITICAL PARTIES AND THE FUTURE

Historically, concern for social order has been associated with conservatives. Nevertheless, the need to reconstruct the private order seems a Democratic opportunity to turn the "social issue" into a Democratic asset. In the first place, established American conservatism rejects government intervention except to punish malefactors and seems to presume a healthy society, able to care for itself if left alone. American conservatism is, in fact, an ossified form of philosophic liberalism, highly individualistic and strongly committed to technological progress and social change. Conservatives bemoan social decay, but they also encourage the forces that promote it. In principle at least, Democrats seem better suited to the use of public power to strengthen the civic bond, encouraging new forms of private order while protecting those parts of the old private order that remain viable. Carter's expressed concern for the family and for ethnic culture could easily coexist with interest in new analogues of the extended family and with ideas of community control.

There are no grounds for believing that this will happen, however. Like the Americans who elected him, Jimmy Carter is divided between his traditional, religious morality and his commitment to scientific management and to the liberal creed that shaped our formal institutions. Many Democrats, moreover, wedded to individualistic ideas of personal liberty, see nothing alarming in the decay of the old order and often applaud its demise. There are fewer reasons to believe that Carter and the Democrats will *rise* to the challenge of an "age of reconstruction" than there are reasons to believe that Republicans will *fail* it.[21] We may, in fact, stand at the beginning of a period of one-party rule not unlike the years during which the Federalist party languished and died and the dominant Jeffersonians stagnated.

In any case, all political parties have an interest in addressing the social issue and in seeking to rebuild the foundations of civic community. The historic bases of party identification are weakening, and the new ties are fragile. Citizens in "limited liability communities" do not make strong partisans.[22] They restrict their trust in parties and leaders as they limit their commitments to their fellow citizens. Strong democratic parties require a strong private order, and democratic government requires strong political parties to make government responsive to citizens and to make citizens devoted to law and the common good.

In fact, however, American political parties have grown weaker. The direct primary, designed to weaken party organization, has now become nearly universal.[23] The Campaign Reform Act gives public money to individual candidates, treating political relationships as bonds between leaders and followers, not as ties between citizens. Moreover, while campaign legislation limits the total amount that a candidate may spend, it permits this money to be spent as the candidate decides. In 1976, both candidates understandably opted to use almost all their limited funds on the mass media, radically reducing efforts to involve citizens and to encourage local organization and participation. This decreased the extent to which the election was a civic and public event. This aspect of the campaign law has been widely criticized, and it seems likely to be corrected. One must hope it will be. As it stands, federal law seems to encourage a politics based almost solely on leaders who relate to followers through the mass media. That is closer to the model of totalitarian parties that it is to traditional democratic ideals.

In 1976, Carter tapped feelings of alienation from the federal government, seen by more and more citizens as a distant, impersonal bureaucracy. Carter's arguments in favor of a reorganized and simplified government that citizens can understand are part of the Jeffersonian tradition. But Jefferson also recognized that citizens need a government which is *responsive*. Today, citizens constantly depend on government, and they have even greater needs for a sense of connection to it and for ways of being heard. Political parties in which citizens are more than spectators are essential to a proper relation between citizen and government.

In fact, political parties are especially vital given our new political anxieties. In 1976, Americans were worried about the most basic aspects of political identity; they were concerned with the social and moral foundations of community, and they felt the need for ties with *each other* as much as or more than they felt the need of ties to Washington. Political parties can themselves—through local organizations and citizen participation—be part of a new network of ties among citizens.

The old limits on government, the mechanical "balances" and statutes designed to keep government out of our lives, are now evidently inadequate. We need government in our lives to strengthen, and in some cases to create, "society." But government that enters our lives so pervasively can easily be despotic without new kinds of restraint. Limited government in 1976 depends less on self-regulated mechanisms and more on citizen-regulated politics. Political parties have done more than express the needs and feelings of citizens. They have educated them in the norms and values of democratic politics. With some justice, George Washington Plunkitt asserted that "the parties built this great country." [24] And the ideal of civic education through revitalized parties is certainly attractive, only eight years from 1984.

Inaugural Address of President Jimmy Carter

For myself and for our nation, I want to thank my predecessor for all he has done to heal our land.

In this outward and physical ceremony we attest once again to the inner and spiritual strength of our nation.

As my high school teacher, Miss Julia Coleman, used to say, "We must adjust to changing times and still hold to unchanging principles."

Here before me is the Bible used in the inauguration of our first President in 1789, and I have just taken the oath of office on the Bible my mother gave me just a few years ago, opened to a timeless admonition from the ancient prophet Micah:

"He hath showed thee, O man, what is good; and what doth the Lord require of thee, but to do justly, and to love mercy, and to walk humbly with thy God." (Micah 6:8)

This inauguration ceremony marks a new beginning, a new dedication within our Government, and a new spirit among us all. A President may sense and proclaim that new spirit, but only a people can provide it.

Two centuries ago our nation's birth was a milestone in the long quest for freedom, but the bold and brilliant dream which excited the founders of our nation still awaits its consummation. I have no new dream to set forth today, but rather urge a fresh faith in the old dream.

Ours was the first society openly to define itself in terms of both spirituality and human liberty. It is that unique self-definition which has given us an exceptional appeal—but it also imposes on us a special obligation, to take on those moral duties which, when assumed, seem invariably to be in our own best interests.

You have given me a great responsibility—to stay close to you, to be worthy of you and to exemplify what you are. Let us create together a new national spirit of unity and trust. Your strength can compensate for my weakness, and your wisdom can help minimize my mistakes.

Let us learn together and laugh together and work together and pray together, confident that in the end we will triumph together in the right.

The American dream endures. We must once again have faith in our country—and in one another. I believe America can be better. We can be even stronger than before.

Let our recent mistakes bring a resurgent commitment to the basic principles of our nation, for we know that if we despise our own Government we have no future. We recall in special times when we have stood briefly, but magnificently, united; in those times no prize was beyond our grasp.

But we cannot dwell upon remembered glory. We cannot afford to drift. We reject the prospect of failure or mediocrity or an inferior quality of life for any person.

Our Government must at the same time be both competent and compassionate.

We have already found a high degree of personal liberty, and we are now struggling to enhance equality of opportunity. Our commitment to human rights must be absolute, our laws fair, our natural beauty preserved; the powerful must not persecute the weak, and human dignity must be enhanced.

We have learned that "more" is not necessarily "better," that even our great nation has its recognized limits and that we can neither answer all questions nor solve all problems. We cannot afford to do everything, nor can we afford to lack boldness as we meet the future. So together, in a spirit of individual sacrifice for the common good, we must simply do our best.

Our nation can be strong abroad only if it is strong at home, and we know that the best way to enhance freedom in other lands is to demonstrate here that our democratic system is worthy of emulation.

To be true to ourselves, we must be true to others. We will not behave in foreign places so as to violate our rules and standards here at home, for we know that this trust which our nation earns is essential to our strength.

The world itself is now dominated by a new spirit. Peoples more numerous and more politically aware are craving and now demanding their place in the sun—not just for the benefit of their own physical condition, but for basic human rights.

The passion for freedom is on the rise. Tapping this new spirit, there can be no nobler nor more ambitious task for America to undertake on this day of a new beginning than to help shape a just and peaceful world that is truly humane.

We are a strong nation and we will maintain strength so sufficient that it need not be proven in combat—a quiet strength based not merely on the size of an arsenal, but on the nobility of ideas.

We will be ever vigilant and never vulnerable, and we will fight our wars against poverty, ignorance and injustice, for those are the enemies against which our forces can be honorably marshaled.

We are a proudly idealistic nation, but let no one confuse our idealism with weakness.

Because we are free we can never be indifferent to the fate of freedom elsewhere. Our moral sense dictates a clearcut preference for those societies which share with us an abiding respect for individual human rights. We do not seek to intimidate, but it is clear that a world which others can dominate with impunity would be inhospitable to decency and a threat to the well-being of all people.

The world is still engaged in a massive armaments race designed to insure continuing equivalent strength among potential adversaries. We pledge perseverance and wisdom in our efforts to limit the world's armaments to those necessary for each nation's own domestic safety. We will move this year a step toward our ultimate goal—the elimination of all nuclear weapons from this earth.

We urge all other people to join us, for success can mean life instead of death.

Within us, the people of the United States, there is evident a serious and purposeful rekindling of confidence, and I join in the hope that when my time as your President has ended, people might say this about our nation:

That we had remembered the words of Micah and renewed our search for humility, mercy and justice;

That we had torn down the barriers that separated those of

different race and region and religion, and where there had been mistrust, built unity, with a respect for diversity;

That we had found productive work for those able to perform it;

That we had strengthened the American family, which is the basis of our society;

That we had insured respect for the law, and equal treatment under the law, for the weak and the powerful, for the rich and the poor;

And that we had enabled our people to be proud of their own Government once again.

I would hope that the nations of the world might say that we had built a lasting peace, based not on weapons of war but on international policies which reflect our own most precious values.

These are not just my goals. And they will not be my accomplishments, but the affirmation of our nation's continuing moral strength and our belief in an undiminished, ever-expanding American dream.

NOTES

Chapter 1. The Nominating Contests and Conventions

1. Candor requires me to admit that one expert, Walter Dean Burnham, did predict the Carter nomination, when he spoke at the meeting of the Northeast Political Science Association on November 13, 1975. Professor Burnham also then predicted Ronald Reagan's nomination by the Republicans.

2. For full accounts of Watergate history, see Theodore H. White, *Breach of Faith* (New York: Atheneum, 1975); and the Staff of the New York Times, *The End of a Presidency* (New York: Bantam, 1974).

3. Clinton Rossiter, *The American Presidency* (New York: Harcourt, Brace, 1960), p. 73.

4. *New York Times*, 24 March 1974, p. 32.

5. The acts' original provisions are listed in *Congressional Quarterly Weekly Report* 32 (5 October 1974): 2691, and the modifications in *Congressional Quarterly Weekly Report* 34 (8 May 1976): 1104–6.

6. An additional 20% may be spent for fund raising. Spending by national, state, and local committees is also excluded from the totals.

7. This movement was predicted, and advocated by Kevin Phillips, *The Emerging Republican Majority* (Garden City, N.Y.: Doubleday Anchor, 1970).

8. *Ripon Society* v. *National Republican Party*, 525 F. 2d 567 (1975), cert. denied 96 S. Ct. 1147 (1976). The existing formula provides three delegates for each electoral vote. To this is added five bonus delegates plus 60% of the electoral vote if the state voted Republican for President, and one bonus vote each if the state last voted Republican for governor, senator, and a majority of the House delegates.

9. Philip Converse et al. "Continuity and Change in American Politics: Parties and Issues in the 1968 Election," *American Political Science Review* 63 (December 1969): 1091.

10. The existence of extensive differences among Democrats is demonstrated by Arthur Miller et al. "A Majority Party in Disarray," *American Political Science Review* 70 (September 1976): 753–78; and Norman Nie et al., *The Changing American Voter* (Cambridge, Mass.: Harvard University Press, 1976), chap. 12.

11. The text of the party charter can be found in *Congressional Quarterly Weekly Report* 32 (14 December 1974): 3334–36.

12. See Austin Ranney, *Curing the Mischiefs of Faction* (Berkeley: University of California Press, 1975).

13. See Theodore H. White, *The Making of the President 1960* (New York: Atheneum, 1961), chaps. 2, 4, 5.

14. Jackson is profiled in *Candidates '76* (Washington, D.C.: Congressional Quarterly, 1976), pp. 44–50. This publication is an excellent guide to the early events of the campaign.

15. See Lewis Chester et al., *An American Melodrama* (New York: Viking, 1969), pp. 158–72.

16. See Gary Hart, *Right From the Start* (New York: Quadrangle, 1973); and William Keech and Donald Matthews, *The Party's Choice* (Washington, D.C.: Brookings Institution, 1976), pp. 144–56.

17. Carter presents an interesting account of these activities in his autobiography, *Why Not the Best?* (New York: Bantam, 1975), chap. 15.

18. See Max Weber, *Politics as a Vocation* (Philadelphia: Fortress Press, 1965), p. 9.

19. *Congressional Quarterly Weekly Report* 34 (17 July 1976): 1933 f.

20. *New York Times,* 29 April 1976, p. 29.

21. *New York Times,* 9 June 1976, p. 21.

22. See the polls reported in *New York Times,* 4 June 1976, p. A12; 20 May 1976, p. 29.

23. The table sources are *Congressional Quarterly Weekly Report* 34 (10 July 1976): 1806 f; idem (24 July 1976): 1987.

24. The poll data are taken from the *Gallup Opinion Index,* no. 129 (April 1976): 4; and idem, no. 133 (August 1976): 6; the *Harris Surveys,* 15 April 1976 and 31 May 1976. The delegate counts are found in the successive weekly issues of *Congressional Quarterly Weekly Report* 34 (1976).

25. William A. Gamson, "Coalition Formation at Presidential Nominating Conventions," *American Journal of Sociology* 68 (September 1962): 157–71.

26. Nie et al., *Changing American Voter,* p. 199.

27. *Gallup Opinion Index,* no. 127 (February 1976): 18.

28. The 1952 roll call, and other historical convention data, may be found in Richard Bain, *Convention Decisions and Voting Records* (Washington, D.C.: Brookings Institution, 1960). Two 1976 votes for other candidates are equally divided in this calculation between Ford and Reagan.

29. Nie et al., *Changing American Voter,* p. 203.

30. *Gallup Opinion Index,* no. 129 (April 1976): 5; and idem, no. 131 (June 1976): 2.

31. *Congressional Quarterly Weekly Report* 34 (10 July 1976): 1808, provides a summary. The table is constructed from the weekly reports.

32. *New York Times,* 20 July 1976, p. 20.

33. Niccolo Machiavelli, *The Prince* (New York: F. S. Crofts, 1947), chap. 17, p. 48.

34. Frank Munger and James Blackhurst, "Factionalism in the National Conventions, 1940–1964: An Analysis of Ideological Consistency in State Delegation Voting," *Journal of Politics* 27 (May 1965): 375–94.

35. *Congressional Quarterly Weekly Report* 34 (21 August 1976): 2314.

36. Finley Peter Dunne, *The World of Mr. Dooley,* ed. Louis Filler (New York: Collier, 1962), p. 50.

37. See "Choosing Vice-Presidents: No Changes Seen," *Congressional Quarterly Weekly Report* 34 (3 July 1976): 1727–30.

38. See "Naming Vice-Presidents: Efforts to Improve System," *Congressional Quarterly Weekly Report* 32 (12 January 1974): 48–50.

39. See Gerald Pomper, "Reforming the Vice-Presidential Nomination," *Public Policy* 2 (Summer 1974): 289–94.

40. James N. Naughton, "Reagan and Credibility," *New York Times,* 30 July 1976, p. A7.

41. *New York Times,* 20 August 1976, p. 1.

42. James I. Lengle and Byron Shafer, "Primary Rules, Political Power, and Social Change," *American Political Science Review* 7 (March 1976): 25–40.

43. See Rowland Evans and Robert Novak, "Jimmy's Labor Tail," *New York Post*, 19 July 1976, p. 23.

44. John H. Britton, "Democratic Convention: Black Gains," *Focus* 4 (July 1976): 3.

45. Texts of the party platforms may be found in *Congressional Quarterly Weekly Report* 34 (17 July 1976): 1913–29; and idem (21 August 1976): 2292–2307.

46. Keech and Matthews, *Party's Choice*, p. 13.

47. For a general critique of television's distortion of political news, see Thomas Patterson and Robert McClure, *The Unseeing Eye* (New York: G. P. Putnam's Sons, 1976), esp. chap. 1.

48. American Political Science Association, Committee on Political Parties, "Toward a More Responsible Two-Party System," *American Political Science Review* 44 (Supplement 1950): 1.

Chapter 2. Issues in the 1976 Presidential Campaign

1. "Text of the Republican Party's 1976 Platform," *Facts on File* 9 (21 August 1976): 602.

2. Ibid.

3. Ibid.

4. Ibid., p. 603.

5. "Transcript of the First Ford-Carter Debate," *Congressional Quarterly Weekly Report* 34 (25 September 1976): 2596.

6. "Text of Democratic Party Platform," *Facts on File* 9 (3 July 1976): 470.

7. Ibid., p. 469.

8. Ibid.

9. Ibid.

10. Ibid., p. 470.

11. Republican Platform, p. 602.

12. Ibid.

13. First Debate, p. 2588.

14. Republican Platform, p. 602.

15. Ibid.

16. Ibid.

17. First Debate, p. 7.

18. Ibid.

19. Quoted in *Time*, 1 November 1976, p. 31.

20. Ibid.

21. Republican Platform, p. 604.

22. Democratic Platform, p. 472.

23. Ibid.

24. Ibid.

25. Ibid.

26. Republican Platform, p. 606.

27. Ibid.

28. *Time*, 1 November 1976, p. 26.

29. Democratic Platform, p. 475.

30. Ibid., p. 474.

31. Ibid.

32. Ibid., p. 475.

33. Ibid.

34. "Transcript of the Second Ford-Carter Debate," *Facts on File* 9 (9 October 1976): 9.

35. Ibid., p. 8.

36. Ibid., p. 9.

37. Ibid.

38. Quoted in *New York Times*, 10 June 1976, p. 42.

Chapter 3. The Presidential Election

1. On the Electoral College, see Neal Pierce, *The People's President* (New York: Simon & Schuster, 1968); and Wallace Sayre and Judith

Parris, *Voting for President* (Washington, D.C.: Brookings Institution, 1970).

2. For Carter, the gamma correlation of state support is .42; for Ford, −.47. Included are all states, whether using delegate selection or preference primaries except, for the Democrats, West Virginia.

3. For the restrictive effects of the campaign finance law, see "Tight Budget for Presidential Candidates," *Congressional Quarterly Weekly Report* 34 (31 July 1976): 2306 f.

4. For details of the decision, see "Campaign Finance: Congress Weighing New Law," *Congressional Quarterly Weekly Report* 34 (7 February 1976): 267–74.

5. See Kathleen A. Frankovic, "The Effect of Religion on Political Attitudes" (Ph.D. thesis, Rutgers University, 1974); and Philip E. Converse et al., "Stability and Change in 1960: A Reinstating Election," in Angus Campbell et al., *Elections and the Political Order* (New York: Wiley, 1966), p. 87 f. A full discussion of ethnic voting in 1972 can be found in the epilogue to the major study of this subject, Mark Levy and Michael Kramer, *The Ethnic Factor* (New York: Simon & Schuster, 1973).

6. See the major study of Jack Bass and Walter DeVries, *The Transformation of Southern Politics* (New York: Basic, 1976).

7. *Washington Post,* 7 November 1976.

8. In this respect, the campaign had the same effect as that described in the first academic voting survey in 1940. See Paul Lazarsfeld et al., *The People's Choice* (New York: Columbia University Press, 1948).

9. See Arthur Miller et al., "A Majority Party in Disarray: Policy Polarization in the 1972 Election," *American Political Science Review* 70 (September 1976): 753–78.

10. *Time,* 15 November 1976, p. 37.

11. *New York Times,* 24 September 1976.

12. *Playboy* 23 (November 1976): 86.

13. *New York Times,* 23 October 1976.

14. David Easton and Jack Dennis, *Children in the Political System* (New York: McGraw-Hill, 1969), chaps. 8, 9.

15. On the effects of the finance law, see "Candidates Find Money Still Matters in 1976," *Congressional Quarterly Weekly Report* 34 (13 March

1976): 553–57. A view that the law actually benefited Carter is found in *New York Times,* 12 November 1976.

16. *New York Times,* 7 October 1976.

17. This interpretation was essentially agreed to by the pollsters for the rival candidates in postelection discussions. See *New York Times,* 6 November 1976, and *Washington Post,* 7 November 1976.

18. See the chart in *Time,* 15 November 1976, p. 19.

19. *New York Times,* 31 October 1976.

20. *Time,* 15 November 1976, p. 35, showed Mondale preferred by a 51–33 margin.

21. *Newsweek,* 15 November 1976, p. 27 f, reporting an ABC News poll.

22. Voters are more likely to cast ballots when they perceive a close election. On this point, see Angus Campbell et al., *The American Voter* (New York: Wiley, 1960), chap. 5.

23. Ibid., pp. 493–98.

24. See Gerald M. Pomper, *Voters' Choice* (New York: Harper & Row, 1975), pp. 100–105; and *New York Times,* 16 November 1976.

25. Theodore H. White, *The Making of the President 1960* (New York: Atheneum, 1961), p. 254.

26. Pomper, *Voters' Choice,* chaps. 8, 9.

27. Norman Nie, Sidney Verba, and John Petrocik, *The Changing American Voter* (Cambridge, Mass.: Harvard University Press, 1976), p. 302.

28. Warren Miller and Teresa Levitan, *Leadership and Change* (Cambridge, Mass.: Winthrop, 1976), p. 165.

29. Walter Dean Burnham analyzed these trends in *Critical Elections and the Mainsprings of American Politics* (New York: Norton, 1970), chap. 6.

30. This is an NBC News estimate, made in its postelection analyses of November 3, 1976.

31. Donald Stokes, "Some Dynamic Elements in Contests for the Presidency," *American Political Science Review* 60 (March 1966): 27–36; and Pomper, *Voters' Choice,* chap. 7.

32. *Newsweek,* 15 November 1976, p. 29.

33. See the preelection poll results in *Newsweek,* 1 November 1976, p. 20 f.

34. Campbell, *American Voter*, chap. 6.

35. William H. Flanigan and Nancy H. Zingale, *Political Behavior of the American Electorate* (3rd ed.; Boston: Allyn & Bacon, 1975), p. 50.

36. Miller and Levitan, *Leadership and Change*, p. 37.

37. Pomper, *Voters' Choice*, p. 163.

38. The gamma correlation of vote and partisanship, on a simple three-point division into Democrats, Independents, and Republicans, is .79. This result can be compared to a 1972 figure of .71.

39. Pomper, *Voters' Choice*, chap. 7.

40. See Richard Boyd, "Popular Control of Public Policy: A Normal Vote Analysis of the 1968 Elections," *American Political Science Review* 66 (June 1972): 435–88; Herbert Weisberg and Jerrold Rusk; "Perceptions of Presidential Candidates: Implications for Electoral Change," *Midwest Journal of Political Science* 16 (August 1972): 388–410. Miller and Levitan, *Leadership and Change*, chap. 7; Miller et al., "Majority Party in Disarray."

41. See Alden S. Raine, *Change in the Political Agenda* (Sage Professional Papers in American Politics, 1976).

42. Miller and Levitan, *Leadership and Change*, p. 127.

43. The concept was first presented by V. O. Key, Jr., in "A Theory of Critical Elections," *Journal of Politics* 17 (February 1955): 3–18. It has since been elaborated by many others, particularly Burnham, *Critical Elections*.

44. These views are presented, respectively, in Kevin Phillips, *The Emerging Republican Majority* (New York: Arlington House, 1969); James Sundquist, *Dynamics of the Party System* (Washington, D.C.: Brookings Institution, 1973); and Burnham, *Critical Elections*, chap. 5.

45. See Paul Beck, "A Socialization Theory of Partisan Realignment," in *The Politics of Future Citizens*, ed. Richard Niemi (San Francisco: Jossey-Bass, 1974), pp. 199–219.

46. Fuller explanation is provided in Gerald Pomper, "Classification of Presidential Elections," *Journal of Politics* 29 (August 1967): 535–66.

47. The 1976 data used are the Democratic percentage of the two-party vote. For 1968, the first correlation is that of the Humphrey percentage of the three-party vote; the second is that of the Humphrey and Wallace combined vote. The states are unweighted. If they are weighted, using number of Representatives as population weights, the results are not greatly changed, with the correlations of the 1976 vote to other elections as follows: 1972, –.12; 1968 (Humphrey), –.14; 1968 (Humphrey and

Wallace), –.66; 1964, –.10; 1960, .63; 1956, .64; 1952, .74; 1948 (Truman), .08; 1948 (Truman and Thurmond), .53; 1944, .52; 1940, .50; 1936, .39; 1932, .43; 1928, .47.

48. Jerome S. Clubb, William H. Flanigan, and Nancy H. Zingale, "Partisan Realignment Since 1960" (Paper presented at the American Political Science Association meetings, Chicago, 1976), p. 31.

Chapter 4. The Congressional Elections and Outlook

1. *Congressional Quarterly Weekly Report* 34 (6 November 1976): 3119.

2. Ibid.

3. Michael Barone, Grant Ujifusa, and Douglas Matthews, *The Almanac of American Politics, 1976* (New York: Dutton, 1975).

4. *Congressional Quarterly Weekly Report* 34 (6 November 1976): 3127.

5. Donald Matthews, *U.S. Senators and Their World* (New York: Vintage, 1960).

6. Ibid., p. 242.

7. *Congressional Quarterly Weekly Report* 34 (9 October 1976): 2823.

8. See V. O. Key, *Politics, Parties and Pressure Groups* (4th ed.; New York: Crowell, 1958), pp. 615–16; and Warren E. Miller, "Presidential Coattails: A Study of Political Myth and Methodology," *Public Opinion Quarterly* 19 (Winter 1955–56): 26–39.

9. *Congressional Quarterly Weekly Report* 34 (6 November 1976): 3135.

10. Nelson W. Polsby, "The Institutionalization of the House of Representatives," *American Political Science Review* 62 (March 1968): 144–68.

11. *Congressional Quarterly Weekly Report* 34 (16 October 1976): 2986.

12. *Congressional Quarterly Weekly Report* 34 (9 October 1976): 2774–75, 2828–29, and 2858–59.

13. *Congressional Quarterly Weekly Report* 34 (6 November 1976): 3136–38.

14. *Congressional Quarterly Weekly Report* 34 (22 May 1976): 1293.

15. *Congressional Quarterly Weekly Report* 34 (16 October 1976): 2986.

16. *Congressional Quarterly Weekly Report* 34 (22 May 1976): 1285.

17. *Congressional Quarterly Weekly Report* 34 (24 January 1976): 169.

18. *Congressional Quarterly Weekly Report* 34 (31 January 1976): 213.

19. See Richard Neustadt, *Presidential Power: The Politics of Leadership* (New York: Wiley, 1960).

20. The Congressional Quarterly Service analyzes presidential messages, remarks at press conferences, and other presidential documents and statements to isolate the presidential position on issues before Congress. Congressional votes are then tabulated in terms of whether the President's position has been sustained or defeated. At the end of the year a percentage score reflecting the proportion of presidential victories is posted. See *Congressional Quarterly Weekly Report* 34 (30 October 1976): 3094.

21. The best analysis of legislative party leadership in the House is Robert L. Peabody, *Leadership in Congress* (Boston: Little, Brown, 1976). See also John Bibby and Roger Davidson, *On Capitol Hill* (2nd ed.; Hinsdale, Ill.: Dryden, 1972), chap. 4. On committees, see Richard F. Fenno, *Congressmen in Committees* (Boston: Little, Brown, 1973), chaps. 1, 2.

22. See *New York Times*, 7 November 1976, p. 34; and *Congressional Quarterly Weekly Report* 34 (6 November 1976): 3125–26.

23. On congressional norms, see Matthews, *U.S. Senators*; see also Richard F. Fenno, Jr., *The Power of the Purse: Appropriations Politics in Congress* (Boston: Little, Brown, 1966); and Roger H. Davidson, *The Role of the Congressman* (New York: Pegasus, 1969).

24. *Congressional Quarterly Weekly Report* 34 (18 September 1976): 2524–27.

25. *Congressional Quarterly Weekly Report* 34 (2 October 1976): 2780.

26. *Congressional Quarterly Weekly Report* 34 (23 October 1976): 3044–45.

27. *Congressional Quarterly Weekly Report* 34 (16 October 1976): 3009–13.

28. On the "subsystem" or "subgovernments," see Randall B. Ripley and

Grace A. Franklin, *Congress, the Bureaucracy and Public Policy* (Homewood, Ill.: Dorsey, 1976). See also the earlier study, J. Lieper Freeman, *The Political Process: Executive Bureau-Legislative Committee Relations* (New York: Random House, 1955).

Chapter 5. State and Local Elections

1. Theodore H. White, *The Making of the President 1960* (New York: Atheneum, 1961), p. 49.

2. *Congressional Quarterly Weekly Report* 34 (13 November 1976): 3162.

3. Ibid.

4. *Congressional Quarterly Weekly Report* 34 (6 November 1976): 3133–34.

5. *Congressional Quarterly Weekly Report* 34 (13 November 1976): 3164.

6. *New York Times*, 4 November 1976, p. 24.

7. Ibid.

8. *Congressional Quarterly Weekly Report* 34 (13 November 1976): 3164.

Chapter 6. The Outlook for the Carter Administration

1. Robert G. Kaiser, "Clash Shakes Carter Transition Team," *Washington Post,* 8 December 1976.

2. Richard F. Fenno, Jr., *The President's Cabinet* (Cambridge, Mass.: Harvard University Press, 1966), p. 51.

3. Hugh Sidey, "The White House Staff vs. The Cabinet: An Interview with Bill Moyers," in *Inside the System*, ed. Charles Peters and John Rothchild (2nd. ed.; New York: Praeger, 1973), p. 39.

4. Christopher Lydon, "A Single-Minded Band Runs the Carter Drive," *New York Times*, 30 May 1976.

5. Emmet John Hughes, *The Living Presidency* (New York: Coward, McCann & Geoghegan, 1973), p. 151.

6. Harry S Truman, *Memoirs, Year of Decisions* (Garden City, N.Y.: Doubleday, 1955), 1:546.

7. Fenno, *President's Cabinet*, p. 248.

8. Gerald M. Pomper, *Elections in America: Control and Influence in Democratic Politics* (New York: Dodd, Mead, 1968), chaps. 7, 8.

9. "Health Insurance: Carter For, Ford Against," *Congressional Quarterly Weekly Report* 34 (9 October 1976): 2917, 2918.

10. Leslie H. Gelb, "Brzezinski Viewed as Key Adviser to Carter," *New York Times*, 6 October 1976.

11. Leslie H. Gelb, "The Kissinger Legacy," *New York Times Magazine*, 31 October 1976, p. 78.

12. Kathleen Teltsch, "Carter Gives Plan for Nuclear Curb," *New York Times*, 14 May 1976; Leslie H. Gelb, "Carter's Nuclear Plan: A Blend of Old and New," *New York Times*, 14 May 1976; and Don Oberdorfer, "Changes in Emphasis Seen in Foreign Policy Under Carter," *Washington Post*, 4 November 1976.

13. In the second debate on October 6, 1976 in San Francisco, Carter took an aggressive stance against oil embargoes by vowing, "If Saudi Arabia should declare an oil embargo against us, then I would consider that an economic declaration of war and I would make sure that the Saudians [*sic*.] understood this ahead of time so that there would be no doubt in their mind." The transcript of the second debate is found in *Congressional Quarterly Weekly Report* 34 (9 October 1976): 2910.

14. Ken Owen, "The Anti-South Africa Squad Behind Jimmy Carter," *The Star* (Johannesburg), 28 October 1976.

15. This position is set forth by Edward R. F. Sheehan, "The Middle Eastern Realities Facing Carter," *New York Times*, 12 November 1976. The Geneva Conference would presumably include the Palestine Liberation Organization whose demands for a secular Arab-Jewish state are unacceptable to Israel. Geneva would also involve a general settlement rather than the succession of bilateral agreements that Israel prefers.

16. Joseph A. Califano, Jr., *A Presidential Nation* (New York: Norton, 1975), p. 27.

17. David E. Rosenbaum, "Is a Rational Bureaucracy a Rational Goal?" *New York Times*, 28 November 1976.

18. U.S., Congress, Senate, *A Resolution to Establish a Temporary Select Committee to Study the Senate Committee System*, 94th Cong., 1st Sess., 1975, S.Res. 109.

19. Seth S. King, "Nation's Mayors Urge Carter to Establish an Urban Policy to Aid Cities and Ask Access to the White House," *New York Times*, 9 November 1976.

20. See Irving L. Janis, *Victims of Groupthink* (Boston: Houghton Mifflin, 1972).

21. For a sympathetic treatment of Johnson's term as vice-president, see Arthur M. Schlesinger, Jr., *A Thousand Days* (Boston: Houghton Mifflin, 1965), pp. 702–7.

22. James David Barber, *The Presidential Character* (Englewood Cliffs, N.J.: Prentice-Hall, 1972), p. 453 f.

23. Ibid., p. 454.

Chapter 7. The Meaning of the Election

1. V. O. Key, Jr., "The Future of the Democratic Party," *Virginia Quarterly* 28 (1952): 161.

2. Kevin Phillips, *The Emerging Republican Majority* (New York: Arlington, 1969).

3. On this period in southern politics, see C. Vann Woodward, *The Origins of the New South, 1877–1913* (Baton Rouge: Louisiana State University Press, 1951); and V. O. Key, *Southern Politics* (New York: Knopf, 1949), pp. 533–54.

4. Key, "Future of the Democratic Party," p. 173; see also Key's *Public Opinion and American Democracy* (New York: Knopf, 1961).

5. The phrase is taken from Jesse Carpenter, *The South as a Conscious Minority* (New York: New York University Press, 1930).

6. Lyndon B. Johnson, *The Vantage Point* (New York: Holt, Rinehart & Winston, 1971), p. 95. Johnson's feelings are especially notable because to many southerners he was more southwestern than southern.

7. On the concept of "critical elections," see Walter Dean Burnham, *Critical Elections and the Mainsprings of American Politics* (New York: Norton, 1970).

8. For example, see J. A. C. Grant, "The Gild Returns to America," *Journal of Politics* 4 (1942): 303–36, 458–77; John Kenneth Galbraith, *American Capitalism: The Concept of Countervailing Power* (Boston: Houghton Mifflin, 1952); Grant McConnell, *Private Power and American Democracy* (New York: Knopf, 1966); and Theodore Lowi, *The End of Liberalism* (New York: Norton, 1969).

9. Samuel Lubell, *The Future of American Politics* (New York: Harper, 1952); see also Lubell's *The Revolt of the Moderates* (New York:

Harper, 1956) and *The Hidden Crisis in American Politics* (New York: Norton, 1970).

10. Richard Centers, "Children of the New Deal: Social Stratification and Adolescent Attitudes," *International Journal of Opinion and Attitude Research* 4 (1950): 315–35.

11. Herbert McClosky et al., "Issue Conflict and Consensus among Party Leaders and Followers," *American Political Science Review* 54 (1960): 406–27, describes the continuing Republican problem.

12. For the concept of the "social issue," see Richard Scammon and Ben Wattenberg, *The Real Majority* (New York: Coward McCann, 1970).

13. William L. Hauser, *America's Army in Crisis* (Baltimore and London: Johns Hopkins University Press, 1973).

14. Nancy R. McWilliams, "Contemporary Feminism, Consciousness-Raising and Changing Views of the Political," in *Women in Politics*, ed. Jane Jaquette (New York: John Wiley, 1974), pp. 157–70.

15. Thomas Paine, *Common Sense and Other Political Writings* (New York: Liberal Arts, 1953), p. 4.

16. L. H. Butterfield, ed., *Adams Family Correspondence* (New York: Atheneum, 1965), 2:20–21.

17. Alexis de Tocqueville, *Democracy in America* (New York: Vintage, 1957), vol. 1, chap. 17.

18. Cited in John Howe, *The Changing Political Thought of John Adams* (Princeton, N.J.: Princeton University Press, 1966), p. 185.

19. *Democracy in America*, vol. 2, bk. 2, chap. 3.

20. Walter Berns, *The First Amendment and the Future of American Democracy* (New York: Basic Books, 1976).

21. The phrase "age of reconstruction" is taken from Karl Mannheim, *Man and Society in an Age of Reconstruction* (New York: Harcourt Brace, 1951).

22. For the concept of "limited liability community," see Scott Greer, "Individual Participation in Mass Society," in *Approaches to the Study of Politics*, ed. R. Young (Evanston: Northwestern University Press, 1958), pp. 329–42.

23. For an extended critique of the primary system, see my essay "Down with the Primaries," *Commonweal* 103 (2 July 1976): 427–29.

24. William Riordan, *Plunkitt of Tammany Hall* (New York: Dutton, 1963).

INDEX

Index compiled by Marc, David, and Miles Pomper.